# The Employee Ownership Manual

Robert Postlethwaite, Solicitor
with Jeremy Gadd

First published November 2019

by Spiramus Press Ltd

102 Blandford Street

London W1U 8AG

Telephone +44 20 7224 0080

www.spiramus.com


© Spiramus Press Ltd


ISBN

9781910151150  Paperback

9781910151570  Digital

British Library Cataloguing-in-Publication Data.

A catalogue record for this book is available from the British Library.


The right of Robert Postlethwaite and Jeremy Gadd to be identified as the authors of this work has been asserted by them in accordance with the Copyright, Designs and Patents Act, 1988.


Printed and bound in Great Britain by Grosvenor Group (Print Services) Ltd

# FOREWORD

**Deb Oxley OBE**

**Chief Executive of the Employee Ownership Association**

Employee ownership is the fastest growing option for business owners seeking a solution to ownership succession as they approach retirement or the next stage of their working life. It provides an accessible, flexible option for every business, regardless of size, sector or location and is no more expensive or difficult to undertake than other ownership succession options such as a trade sale or a management buyout. Importantly it also has the potential to deliver more value and benefits; to the founder owner, the employees, the customers, the suppliers and the location in which the business is located.

However, whilst its adoption is increasing in popularity, especially with SME and family business owners, the advisory marketplace remains behind the curve. We need more accountants, lawyers and funders to appreciate and understand this innovative business model so that they are best placed to offer advice and support to their clients and to help elevate employee ownership into the mainstream.

Employee ownership does not rely on benevolence or charity; most businesses that become employee owned are limited companies, run for profit, commercially astute and their transition involves the founding owners receiving fair market value.

I whole-heartedly welcome this new book – *The Employee Ownership Manual*. It delivers exactly what is required now to educate and inform more business owners and their advisors about the 'why', the 'what' and the 'how' of employee ownership.

It is a perfect example of a 'manual' as Robert Postlethwaite and Jeremy Gadd guide the reader through each stage in a logical and comprehensive way, offering advice and insight, based on their hands on, extensive experience of supporting many businesses to navigate the employee ownership journey.

I am proud that the Employee Ownership Association has been leading the campaign for more employee ownership for 40 years. over that time the sector has grown significantly – indeed, since 2012, at a rate of approximately 10% per annum. However, there is still more to do until employee ownership is embedded in the business and political mainstream. When that happens, books like this will no longer be necessary; until then, I welcome every opportunity to share advice and information with business owners, their accountants, lawyers, funders and other advisers so that over time, every one of them can realise the potential of employee ownership.

In the meantime, anyone wishing to uncover more stories of and advice about employee ownership should visit the Employee Ownership Association website at:
 www.employeeownership.co.uk.

# Acknowledgements

Writing this book has only been possible with the help of several people. In no particular order, grateful thanks are extended to Judith Harris, Pam Farrance, Toby Locke, Alison Stevens, Anne-Marie Clift, Deb Oxley, David Reuben and to Carl Upsall of Spiramus.

Thank you also for your support and encouragement to Rosie Postlethwaite, Katherine Postlethwaite, Alison Roberts, Julian Roberts, Mike Roberts, Tom Roberts, Peter Clift, Caroline Creaby and Margaret Clift. And last but not least, thank you so much to Roger Postlethwaite who showed me how difficult concepts could often be explained simply and clearly. How else would I ever have passed my Physics exams as a teenager? I hope that we have succeeded in doing that in this book.

# Contents

# Introduction: how to use this book

This book is intended to meet a range of different needs and to cater for different levels of knowledge about employee ownership. If you are considering making your company employee-owned or you are advising someone going through that process, and in either case are new to the topic, you can build up your knowledge levels from Chapter 1. Alternatively, the book can be used as a reference work if you have a particular question to answer.

Some parts of the book will not be relevant to every reader. For example, several chapters consider how employees can acquire shares personally: these will not be relevant to companies which intend their employee ownership only to be through an employee trust.

The book is intended as practical guide rather than a highly detailed technical treatise. Its priority is to explain key issues in an accessible fashion and to raise awareness of where further exploration and advice may be important.

**Chapter 1** looks at the background to employee ownership and why companies choose to become employee-owned.

**Chapter 2** – Employee trusts are a key part of the structure of most employee-owned companies, as outlined in this chapter. Individual share ownership is also introduced here, as some employee-owned companies combine ownership by an employee trust (which usually holds the majority of the company's shares) with direct, individual ownership of shares by employees.

**Chapter 3** goes more deeply into how employee trusts work and how the role of trustees as owners interacts with the role of the company's directors.

**Chapter 4** – The key steps and decisions that will need to be made in establishing an employee trust are considered.

**Chapter 5** starts to look in more detail at individual share ownership, in particular the ways in which employees can acquire shares personally, and provides a summary of the tax reliefs that are available for individual employees acquiring shares in their company.

**Chapter 6** – Employee ownership trusts are a particular kind of employee trust, bringing particular tax reliefs. This chapter considers these tax reliefs and the various conditions which must be satisfied.

**Chapter 7** – Many companies become employee-owned through the existing owners transferring their shares to an employee trust. This chapter looks at how to plan ownership succession in this way and some key questions that will need to be considered.

**Chapter 8** – An employee ownership trust deed is likely to form the structural core of most employee-owned companies. This chapter explains the key provisions that it will commonly include.

**Chapter 9** considers the people issues which arise in a transition to employee ownership, and has been written by Jeremy Gadd.

*The next five chapters look in more detail at how employees can acquire shares individually and may be of value to companies wishing to include individual share ownership alongside trust ownership.*

*Chapters 10 and 11 look at two tax-advantaged all-employee share schemes.*

**Chapter 10** – The Share Incentive Plan (SIP) enables employees to purchase shares or receive free shares, in each case with relief against income tax. The SIP is an all-employee share scheme, which means that all employees must be allowed to participate in any offer of shares. This chapter looks at the statutory requirements for operating a SIP and how it works in practice.

**Chapter 11** – Save As You Earn (SAYE) options is another form of all-employee share scheme, under which employees can be granted options to acquire shares in the future and those employees who participate will save a monthly amount towards the option exercise price. This chapter considers how SAYE options work.

*Chapters 12 and 13 look at tax-advantaged share schemes which do not need to involve all employees:*

**Chapter 12** looks at Enterprise Management Incentive (EMI) options. For companies wishing to create personal share ownership for their key people, EMI options will often be the best place to start. There are particular eligibility requirements for EMI options. These are considered in this chapter, which also discusses the key elements of an EMI scheme, and offers suggestions as to how EMI options can be structured.

**Chapter 13** – An alternative to EMI options is the Company Share Option Plan (CSOP). This chapter considers how the CSOP works.

**Chapter 14** looks at other ways in which employees can acquire shares personally.

*Chapters 15 to 20 consider other legal, regulatory and taxation issues.*

**Chapter 15** – Where employees are to acquire shares (or cash) from an employee trust, it is important to ensure that this is structured in a way which does not fall foul of tax anti-avoidance rules which were introduced to counter what is commonly referred to as *disguised remuneration.* This chapter looks at these provisions and how to keep on the right side of them. Failure to do so could result in a charge to income tax and National Insurance on the value of assets even though an employee has not acquired any definite ownership rights over them.

**Chapter 16** sweeps up some other legal and regulatory matters not directly covered in previous chapters.

**Chapter 17** covers data protection requirements.

**Chapter 18** covers phantom shares.

**Chapter 19** looks at the interaction between corporation tax, employee trusts and different individual employee share schemes.

**Chapter 20** – There are a number of registration and filing requirements with HM Revenue and Customs and the Registrar of Companies. This chapter considers these and some continuing administration requirements and summarises the accounting treatment of employee trusts and employee share schemes.

# 1 What is employee ownership and why introduce it?

## 1.1 What is employee ownership?

This book is about a form of ownership under which all or most employees together hold a significant stake in the business they work for. We refer to this as *employee ownership* and describe businesses owned in this way as *employee-owned.*

In this book, *employee ownership* is distinguished from another way in which employees can be involved in business ownership, usually called an *employee share scheme*, which does not of itself involve ownership of a significant stake.

An employee share scheme can play an important role in a company's performance and growth, but is very different from employee ownership, principally because it will on its own rarely, if ever, involve employees as a whole having control of, or significant influence over, their company.

That said, it is possible for a company to be both employee-owned and also to have an employee share scheme. This is explored further in this book.

### (a) An employee share scheme?[1]

This is an arrangement in which a percentage of a company's shares are reserved for its employees, who will (either immediately or at some point in the future) hold shares alongside other shareholders – typically founders and/or outside investors – who together own the majority of the company.

-------

[1] It can also have a variety of other descriptions, including employee share plan, employee stock plan and employee share ownership plan. And sometimes the same term can be used by different people to describe very different things. Don't just rely on the name to understand what the arrangement is, but always delve into how it actually involves employees in ownership, who benefits and how much of the business is owned in this way.

The percentage reserved for employees will vary from company to company and could range from under 5% to 20%, occasionally more.

An employee share scheme will typically involve participating employees acquiring shares directly, either by purchase or gift, or by being granted options to acquire shares at a future date and at a fixed price.

### (i) Which employees participate in their company's employee share scheme?

Participation can be limited to senior leadership team members and other key people or it can involve all of a company's employees. Private companies have tended to focus on the former, whereas many listed companies have employee share schemes for both categories.[2]

A company could have an employee share scheme involving ownership by:

- *senior leadership and key people only*
- *both senior leadership/key people and all employees*
- *all employees only.*

### (b) Employee ownership

Employee ownership takes things further than an employee share scheme. It always involves all or most of a company's employees and – here is the critical difference – it also involves a significant stake in the company being owned by the employees.

In most companies that describe themselves as employee-owned, more than 50% of the shares will typically be held by or on behalf of employees, but there are some where the percentage is lower. As employee ownership is in many ways at least as much about

---

[2] According to HM Revenue and Customs statistics published in June 2019, approximately 2.9 million UK employees purchased shares in their employer company in 2018 under a Share Incentive Plan (SIP), involving around 800 companies. It is likely that the vast majority of those companies were listed and that they also had one or more employee share schemes for their directors or key people only.

EMPLOYEE OWNERSHIP

culture and engagement as numbers of shares held, it is important not to attach undue weight to percentages, but for the purpose of this book an ownership stake for employees of at least 25% is assumed.

## 1.2   Why employee ownership?

It sounds obvious, doesn't it? If you share the rewards of a successful business with its employees, those employees will have a powerful incentive to engage in their business and work – together – in ways which improve its performance. What results is a "win-win" from whichever angle you view it:

- *improved productivity and competitiveness*
- *increased wealth for employees through their company's economic success*
- *enhanced returns for investors*
- *a stronger economy through more resilient companies with a keen focus on the longer term.*

That is the theory – but is it matched by the reality?

There is significant academic and other evidence of the benefits of employee ownership.

In 2018, the Ownership Effect Inquiry published a report, *The Ownership Dividend*,[3] which found that employee ownership delivered benefits for business, individuals and the wider economy. For example, sales by employee-owned companies were found to have grown by 3% more than non-employee-owned companies in 2017.

According to the Employee Ownership Association, in the same year employee-owned companies experienced a 6.4% growth in productivity compared with 3.4% for other companies.

---

[3] The Ownership Effect Inquiry, commissioned in 2017 by the Employee Ownership Association, the John Lewis Partnership and the EAGA Trust, delivered its findings, *The Ownership Dividend*, in June 2018. www.theownershipeffect.co.uk

Several longitudinal studies of the impact of employee ownership on business performance have been undertaken in the USA. They tend to show improved performance in companies which have a leadership style compatible with employee ownership, which essentially means one that fosters collaboration, listens to employees and is participative rather than autocratic.[4]

If you talk to people from employee-owned companies, you will often hear of significant performance improvements following their transition to employee ownership:

> *"In our first year since becoming employee-owned, our revenues grew by 50%. Employee ownership has unleashed an extraordinary latent energy and drive in our business".*

This is perhaps at the upper range of employee ownership success. Not every company will enjoy such a dramatic performance effect from becoming employee-owned. And every business looking to enjoy an employee ownership dividend will have to work at it; it won't just happen. But the evidence is clear: if you want your company to improve its performance, you should take a good look at employee ownership.

## 1.3    Employee ownership and an employee share scheme?

A company can be both employee-owned and have an employee share scheme. The two can work alongside each other, as illustrated here:

---

[4] For example, see Joseph Blasi, Douglas Kruse, and Dan Weltmann, "Firm Survival and Performance in Privately-Held ESOP Companies, *Sharing Ownership, Profits, and Decision-Making in the 21st Century* (Advances in the Economic Analysis of Participatory & Labor-Managed Firms, Volume 14, 2013, pp.109-124.

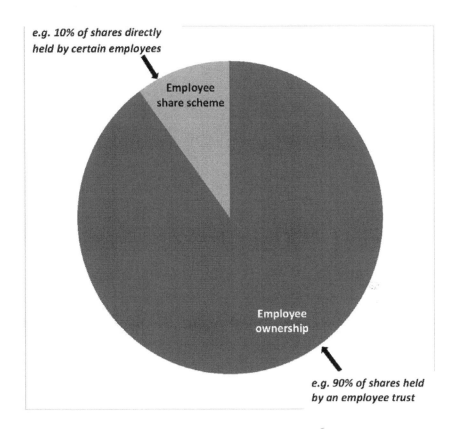

e.g. 10% of shares directly held by certain employees

Employee share scheme

Employee ownership

e.g. 90% of shares held by an employee trust

**To recap:**

- A company can say it is employee-owned when a significant proportion of its shares are held by or on behalf of all its employees.
- An employee share scheme is normally different – it is an arrangement where any number of shares (or share options) are held by employees directly. This could be a relatively small holding and may be held either by key employees only or all employees.
- It is possible for a company to be both employee-owned and to have an employee share scheme.
- Research suggests that companies which are employee-owned outperform those which are not.

## 2 Creating employee ownership

In this chapter we consider different ways in which employee ownership can be structured and the principal situations when a company might become employee-owned (or an existing company might transition to employee ownership). To some degree, the former will often be determined by the latter.

### 2.1 What does an employee-owned company look like?

At first sight, the simplest way of creating employee ownership would be to arrange for all employees to acquire shares, either purchasing them, receiving them free or perhaps being granted options to acquire them later. The total number of shares held by employees would be significant – at least 25% of the company.

Whilst this does sometimes happen, it is often difficult to make individual employee share acquisition work in practice. There is a range of reasons, explored in more detail in Chapter 5, one of which is simply that there is a more straightforward alternative.

In the majority of employee-owned companies in the United Kingdom a significant proportion, often a majority and sometimes all of the shares, will be held in a trust on behalf of employees: an *employee trust*.

### 2.2 An employee trust

Before explaining an *employee trust*, let us look at what a trust is in general terms.

In essence, a trust describes an arrangement under which property is outwardly owned by one or more persons, but where there is an underlying legal duty on those persons to use that property for the benefit of others and not themselves. The trust was originally an English legal creation, but it has now found its way into the legal systems of many other countries.

Believed by many legal historians to have been created in the twelfth century, the trust's origins may be related to the crusades. When a landowner departed to fight in a crusade, it was common to transfer ownership of his land to another person to manage the estate and collect income, on the understanding that if the landowner was fortunate enough to return, it would then be transferred back to him. In some cases a returning crusader would meet with a refusal to do so: *"You gave it to me when you rode off, and it's mine now".* Initially the courts refused to assist, but it become possible to apply to the Lord Chancellor, whose court (the Court of Chancery) would declare that it was unconscionable for the original landowner to be deprived of his property in this way.

So was born the law of trusts. The landowner had trusted someone to hold his land while he was away, and the courts would say that that landowner (the beneficiary of the trust) should be regarded as the true owner.

A legal structure created in the twelfth century to address a problem very much of that time has, over subsequent centuries, turned out to be of significant practical value in a range of other situations. One of the most recent is the advent of employee ownership. Where shares in a company are held in an employee trust, they are owned by a small group of individuals (*trustees*), who are under a legal duty that requires any benefit from their ownership to pass to the employees, rather than being enjoyed by the trustees themselves. It is the employees who benefit from the trust, and so they are called *beneficiaries*.

So, if the company pays a profit share to the trust as a dividend, the trustees will either pass that on to the trust's beneficiaries[5] or they may retain it in the trust to be used in some other way in the future (for example, to purchase more shares if they do not already hold 100% of the company) as long as they consider that is for the benefit of the beneficiaries. If the company is ever sold, it will be the trust that sells the shares and receives the sale proceeds, which will

---

[5] In practice, however, the trustees will often agree to waive their entitlement to a dividend, on the basis that the company will instead make payments directly to employees as a bonus. This avoids the payment being taxed twice, once when received by the trust and then again when received by employees.

normally then be shared between the employees after payment of sale expenses and any taxation.

Employees of a company owned by an employee trust may also enjoy non-financial benefits. For example, many employee-owned companies (and all of those that wish to be successful) will foster a culture of collaboration and positive purpose, intended to lead to a positive business impact through employees who are motivated and engaged in their business. It will often be part of the role of an employee trust to encourage this.

Why does a trust so often form a key, or the only, part of a company's employee ownership? The main reason is that it is simpler to operate compared with individual employee share ownership.

## 2.3   The main types of employee trust

Under United Kingdom taxation and trust law, there are two main kinds of employee trust.

### (a)  Employee benefit trust

The *employee benefit trust* has its origins in the mid-20th century. It is a fully discretionary trust, in that the trustees have wide scope to decide how they should use the trust's assets (normally cash and/or shares) to benefit employees, and which employees are to benefit.

The trustees of an employee benefit trust could exercise their powers to confer benefit on a small group of senior employees, for example by giving them shares or options to acquire shares or by making cash bonus payments. As with all trusts, the trustees of an employee benefit trust have a duty to act in the best interests of the trust's beneficiaries. Since invariably all or most employees of a company with an employee benefit trust will be beneficiaries of that trust, if benefit is conferred on a narrow group of employees it will be important for the trustees to justify this. One example of how that might be done is the company's independent remuneration committee (or board of directors so long as they do not have a conflict of interest) of the company that established the trust (the *settlor*) making a recommendation to the trustees as to how benefit should be conferred.

## (b) Employee ownership trust

The *employee ownership trust* can be considered as a subset of the employee benefit trust. It is also a discretionary trust but the trustees' scope to exercise discretion is significantly narrower.

The employee ownership trust, often abbreviated to **EOT**, was created by the Finance Act 2014, with the intention of encouraging more companies to become employee-owned. The legislation brought in two new tax reliefs, but with conditions to ensure that the result was true, widespread employee ownership rather than ownership concentrated in the hands of a small proportion of employees.

## (c) The tax reliefs

There are two principal tax reliefs associated with employee ownership trusts:

- *relief against CGT for the owner or owners of the Company's shares, on a sale to an employee ownership trust; and*
- *payment of bonuses free of income tax to employees of a company owned by an employee ownership trust.*

These are covered in more detail in Chapter 6 but are briefly summarised below.

The *CGT relief* is intended to encourage owners of an established company who are seeking to retire to sell to an employee ownership trust. The way it works is that if an employee ownership trust acquires more than 50% of the shares in a company, those who sell their shares to the trust will be exempt from CGT.

Under the *income tax relief*, employees of a company that is more than 50% owned by an employee ownership trust may receive an annual bonus of up to £3,600 free of income tax (but still subject to National Insurance).

These tax reliefs will only be available if the conditions laid down by the legislation are satisfied.

These are summarised below. The summary is an overview only. For a fuller description, please go to Chapter 6.

## (i) Capital gains tax relief on a sale to an employee ownership trust

| Condition | Comment |
|---|---|
| The employee ownership trust must acquire more than 50% of the company's shares and must control the company | As the CGT relief is intended to encourage companies to move to majority employee ownership, this is an essential requirement |
| The company must be a *trading company* (or the holding company of a trading group) | The company must operate some kind of trade. So if, for example, it is an investment vehicle (earning its revenues from investments in shares, property, or bank deposits) it will not be a trading company. Even if it does actually trade as well, if its non-trading activities represent 20% or more of its activities, it may not qualify as a trading company |
| Any benefit received by employees from the trust must be for *all employees* | The purpose behind the tax reliefs for employee ownership trusts is to encourage employee ownership for all employees, so the trust deed must stipulate that all employees are to share in any benefit conferred by the trust. It is possible, however, to exclude employees who have not completed a qualifying period of employment (up to twelve months) |
| Any benefit from the trust to employees must be on the *same terms* | This means either:<br>• Each employee receives the same amount; or<br>• Employees receive different amounts depending on their remuneration, length of service or hours worked (or a combination of those factors) |
| If the person claiming the relief held 5% or more of the company in the previous twelve months, the *participator fraction* must not be more than 2/5.<br>In summary, the participator fraction is: | According to HM Revenue and Customs: "The purpose of this requirement is to guard against relief being given to individuals who had a substantial shareholding in the company in circumstances where they, along with other claimants, made up a significant proportion of the business's workforce before and after |

| | |
|---|---|
| Shareholders holding at least 5% who are directors or employees + employees or directors related to them DIVIDED BY Total number of employees | the creation of the EOT" |
| Neither the person claiming the relief nor any relative claimed relief in any earlier year in relation to any disposal of shares in the same company or any member of the same group | Clearly this is designed to prevent an individual claiming CGT relief more than once in respect of the same company (or another company in the same group) |
| No loans to beneficiaries | An employee ownership trust may not make a loan to any beneficiary. This is likely to be because in the past attempts have been made to avoid income tax by employee trusts making loans to individual employees |

## (ii)    *Paying income tax free bonuses*

| Condition | Comment |
|---|---|
| An employee ownership trust must hold more than 50% of the company's shares (or the shares in the company's holding company) | As with the CGT relief, this condition is founded upon the goal of encouraging companies to become majority employee-owned |
| All employees in the company (or in a group of companies) must be eligible to receive an income tax free bonus | As with the CGT relief, this is to ensure that income tax free bonuses are paid to all, not just a selected group. However, an eligibility requirement of up to twelve months can be set |
| Income tax free bonus payments must be paid on the same terms | As with the CGT relief, either each employee must receive the same bonus or differing amounts according to remuneration, length of service or hours worked (or a combination) |
| The employer company must be a trading company | As with the CGT relief, this is to ensure that the income tax relief is not available |

| | |
|---|---|
| (or a member of a trading group) | to companies which are simply investment vehicles |
| The payment must not be regular wages or salary | This is to ensure that the tax relief is used for genuine bonuses only and not as a way to avoid income tax on an employee's normal pay |
| Whilst a bonus can be paid to a former employee or to the estate of a deceased employee, this must not be more than twelve months after the employment ceased or the employee died | The policy behind this is to ensure that the tax relief can only be enjoyed by individuals who have a current or recent employment relationship with the company |
| The payment must not be under a "salary sacrifice" arrangement (that is, an agreement to give up regular wages or salary in return for a bonus) | This is also to ensure that the tax relief is available only for genuine bonuses |
| The ratio of directors to total employees must not exceed 2/5 | This is similar to the CGT relief ratio requirement, and its purpose is to ensure that the income tax relief is not available to companies with only a small number of employees |
| The company must not be a *"service company"* | A service company is a company whose business is providing the services of people employed by it mainly to persons who control it, but who are not members of the same group |
| £3600 maximum bonus per employee per year | When the employee ownership trust tax reliefs were under development, a Treasury condition was to limit the cost to the public purpose through this limit |

## 2.4   When can a company become employee-owned?

Employee ownership will either be created at the beginning of a company's life or through an *established company* changing to become employee owned.

## (a) Employee ownership in a new business

The founders of a new company may decide that they want it to be employee-owned from inception. If they choose trust ownership, the trust might be an employee ownership trust or an employee benefit trust, which will either own the entire company or share the ownership with individual founders and/or external investors.

The diagrams which follow show a number of different ownership permutations. There are others and these are examples only.

*100% ownership by an employee ownership trust*

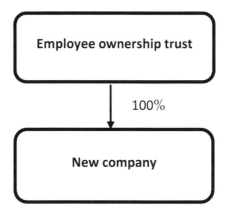

*Majority ownership by an employee ownership trust, minority by an investor*

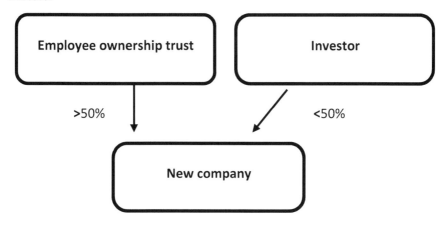

*Majority ownership by an employee ownership trust, minority by individual employees*

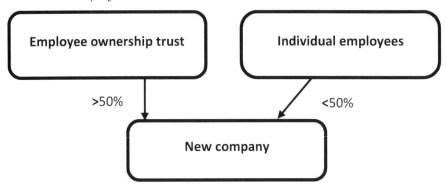

Where delivery of a public service is to be taken over by an employee-owned company under contract, so that the public sector body which was providing that service will instead become a commissioner of the service, it is common for the new provider to be established under employee trust ownership. However, this structure is by no means the preserve of public sector service providers, as it is well suited to the needs of any new business that wishes to be employee-owned.

**(b) Employee ownership in an established business**
Here are some further examples of employee ownership, this time in an established business.

*Existing owners (founders) transfer entire company to employee ownership*

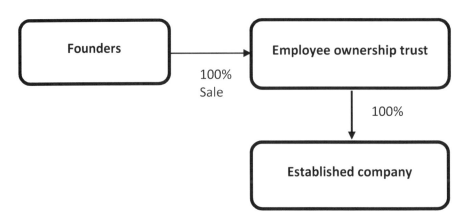

*Existing owners (founders) transfer a majority holding only*

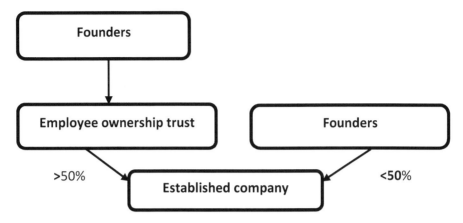

Many employee-owned companies come into being because existing owners wish to retire and, having considered possible alternative ways of realising the value of their shares, elect for employee ownership.

There are several reasons why company owners choose this route. Sometimes the starting point is defensive (for example *"We can't find a buyer"* or *"We could sell but we don't trust any new owner to value our business or its employees"*) but invariably where employee ownership is chosen it will be because it is felt to be in the best interests of the company long term. Whilst exemption from CGT makes selling to an employee ownership trust more tax efficient for retiring owners than any alternative, if a company is going to succeed under employee ownership it is important to be confident that it will lead to engaged and motivated employees and that those taking over the leadership are committed to adapting to this new structure.

## 2.5   Creating an employee trust

### (a)  Trust deed

For a company wishing to create an employee trust (whether an employee benefit trust or an employee ownership trust), the first step will be to prepare a *trust deed*. This document will be signed as a deed by the company and the first trustees. As a minimum it will typically:

- *appoint trustees (and say how successors should be appointed);*
- *say who are the trust's beneficiaries (employees, or employees who have been with the company for a minimum period, and sometimes also including former employees and dependants of deceased employees);*
- *set out what powers the trustees have (because their basic legal powers are limited); and*
- *record the transfer by the company to the trust of an initial cash sum (this need not be significant), because for a trust to be created it must own some property.*

In practice, a trust deed will normally contain other provisions as well.

Once the trust deed has been signed and some initial property transferred to it (normally a nominal amount of £100), the trust exists.

### (b) Acquiring shares

The next step will be for the trust to acquire shares in the company. How it does so will depend on whether the employee trust is being established as part of *a new company* or to take over ownership of *an existing company from owners wishing to retire.*

### (i) *New company*

Typically, the employee trust will subscribe for new shares in the company. In other words, that company will create new shares and agree that the trust becomes their owner.

The trust will have to pay for the shares. In a new company with no trading history, profits or assets, it is unlikely that these shares will have any value, meaning that the financial cost to the trust may not be significant. One possible exception is where the company is bringing in other shareholders as investors. In that situation, if investors have paid a certain price for shares in the company (or have indicated a willingness to do so) in the belief that the company will grow and generate profits and a return on their investment, shares in the company may have a significant market value. In either situation, trustees should consider obtaining a professional valuation of the shares which they are contemplating acquiring.

The diagram below shows how an employee trust can be funded by the company to acquire new shares:

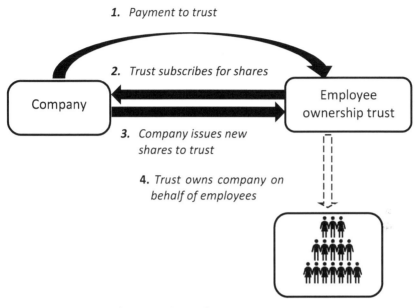

1. *Payment to trust*

2. *Trust subscribes for shares*

Company

Employee ownership trust

3. *Company issues new shares to trust*

4. *Trust owns company on behalf of employees*

### (ii) *Change of ownership of an existing company*

Here the employee trust will be purchasing existing shares and the process looks a little different.

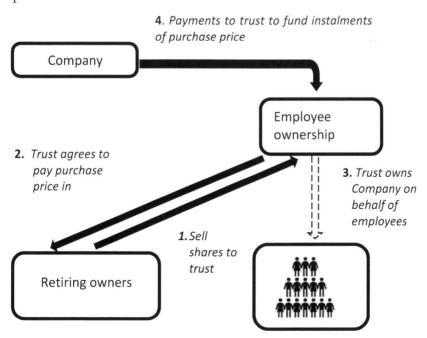

4. *Payments to trust to fund instalments of purchase price*

Company

Employee ownership

2. *Trust agrees to pay purchase price in*

3. *Trust owns Company on behalf of employees*

1. *Sell shares to trust*

Retiring owners

Where an employee trust is purchasing existing shares, it is generally recommended to create a written contract between the trustees (as buyers) and the existing shareholders (as sellers) to set out the terms of the purchase. As a minimum, this will identify the shares being sold and the purchase price and may also include other terms. This is considered in more detail in Chapter 7.

### (c) Trust as shareholder

The result of each of these processes is that the employee trust will have become a shareholder in the Company. It may hold all the shares or it may have one or more co-shareholders, depending on the circumstances.

Other shareholders may include founders who have retained some of their shares, individual employees or investors.

## 2.6  Individual share ownership

An alternative form of employee share ownership is for shares to be held by employees individually, rather than the shares being held on their behalf in an employee trust.

Whilst this structure is sometimes seen, it is unusual. Where a company is to be employee-owned *from its inception*, it will be simpler to establish an employee trust to hold shares for employees. As the company grows and more employees join, they will automatically become beneficiaries of the trust. This is far simpler than having to implement the various steps that would be needed for each employee to become a shareholder personally. This approach would unavoidably require the company to approve the issue of new shares to each employee and generate documentation to record this. Personal employee share ownership would also either require each employee to pay for their shares or involve the use of a tax advantaged share scheme to enable the shares to be acquired free or at a discounted price without adverse tax consequences.

Employee ownership through a trust avoids these complexities, although it is possible that over the longer term the company may decide that it is worth combining trust ownership with some personal share ownership (see Chapter 5).

The same issues apply where a company's route to employee ownership is *succession*, but here there are additional reasons why it makes sense to use an employee trust. Imagine a company with four shareholders wishing to retire and eighty employees. To transfer ownership from those shareholders to the employees personally would require a web of personal contracts between each selling shareholder and a group of employees. (In its very simplest version, if all employees were to take over as shareholders each retiring shareholder would have contracts with twenty employees). As if this is not enough of a practical obstacle, there is also the question of whether individual employees would be able to afford the purchase price. It is highly unusual for most employees to have much, if any, spare cash to fund a share purchase in this way.

The only practical way to transfer ownership to employees is to have a single purchaser in the form of an employee trust, which in the above example would mean a single contract between the trust and the four selling shareholders. The trust would be funded by the company to pay the purchase price, normally over a period of years (see Chapter 7).

**To recap:**
- Although employee ownership can be structured through creating individual share ownership, it is simpler and far more common for an employee trust to hold the shares on behalf of the employees, at least initially. Once the trust has acquired its shares, over the longer term it may transfer some of them to individual employees.
- There are two forms of employee trust: the employee benefit trust and the employee ownership trust (EOT). Where a company becomes majority owned by an EOT, employees can be paid annual bonuses free of income tax (£3600 per employee per year maximum) and those shareholders who sell their shares to the EOT can claim exemption from CGT.
- Employee ownership can be created when a new company is formed, so it is employee-owned from its inception, or under a plan for ownership succession.

- An employee trust is created by the company and those who are going to operate the trust – its trustees – signing a trust deed.
- Once the trust has been established, it will acquire ownership of the company either by subscribing for new shares (in the case of a new company) or by purchasing shares from retiring shareholders.
- An employee trust may hold all the shares in a company, or it may hold a significant number (normally a majority if it is an EOT) alongside other kinds of shareholder.

# 3 Employee trusts: how they work

## 3.1 What this chapter covers

This chapter will explain, for any company that is wholly or majority owned by an employee trust, how the trust works, who runs it and what is its role. It also considers the general legal duties of the trustees and compares these with those of a company's directors.

## 3.2 What property does the employee trust hold?

The main *property* held by an employee trust will be the shares in the company that it has acquired from former shareholders. It is unlikely that any other property will be held by the trust, perhaps other than small amounts of cash.

By holding all, or a majority of, the company's shares, it will control the company. It will have the right to decide who will act as the company's directors and, if it holds 75% or more of the total shares, it will have a greater degree of control, enabling it, for example, to make changes to the company's constitution (*articles of association*).

It will also have a right to receive a percentage of any profits of the company to be paid to shareholders, equal to the size of its shareholding. If the company is ever sold or liquidated[6], it will be entitled to a share of any payout on the same basis.

## 3.3 Who runs the trust?

The trust will be run by its *trustees*. It can have either a number of individual trustees, or a single trustee which would be a company formed specially for the purpose of acting as trustee. In the latter situation, it is the directors of that *trustee company* who in effect will be the trustees.

---

[6] On the liquidation (or winding up) of a company, it stops trading, its assets are used to pay off its debts and, if anything is left over, it is normally paid out to shareholders. Many liquidations are *insolvent,* which means the value of debts is greater than the value of assets, so there is nothing to pay to shareholders. In some circumstances, however, a liquidation can be *solvent* and shareholders will receive a payout.

There are two main reasons why a trustee company is often preferred over individual trustees.

First, if there is a change of trustee, this is easier to process administratively if there is a *trustee company*. A short form needs to be filed at Companies House to record a trustee's termination and a separate form is filed to record the appointment of a new trustee. Where instead an *individual trustee* is stepping down and a successor is being appointed, a formal deed of retirement and appointment is required to be signed, which is a little more involved.

Second, acting as a trustee through being a director of a trustee company confers on the individual some additional protection from limited liability in case they make an error.

In the remainder of this book, wherever the word trustee is used, it can mean either an *individual trustee* or a director of a trustee company.

There are no specific rules as to who may be a trustee of an employee trust (whether the trust is an employee benefit trust or an employee ownership trust). However, there are some recommended practical considerations:

- *Ideally, no directors of the trading company should also be trustee of the employee trust which owns a majority of that trading company. This is to avoid potential conflicts of interest, since part of the trustee's role will be to ensure that the company's directors are performing effectively as leaders. This is a counsel of perfection and may not always be possible. However, there may sometimes be arguments in favour of one trustee being drawn from the company's directors, for example their knowledge of the company and its marketplace. It is recommended, however, that at most a minority of trustees should be directors of the company.*
- *Where an employee trust is acquiring shares in an established company as part of an ownership succession plan, retiring shareholders may wish to become trustees. This can work well but it will generally be important to ensure that they do not comprise a majority of trustees. Otherwise, there is a risk of HM Revenue and*

*Customs taking the view that the retiring shareholders have not given up control of the company. The likely result would then be their sale proceeds being subject to income tax rather than CGT, meaning a significantly higher tax payment.*

- *It is very common for the trustees of an employee trust to include at least one employee and equally common for that employee trustee to be chosen by the employees as a whole. Where the company does not immediately feel ready to organise an election, a compromise is for the first employee trustee(s) to be individuals appointed by the company's directors for a limited period (typically, three years), after which any successor is appointed by employees.*

- *There is often a benefit in one of the trustees being from outside the company, perhaps an individual with a business background or a professional adviser such as a lawyer or accountant. Having an independent trustee reduces the likelihood of trustees lapsing into "groupthink" and can bring a fresh, sometimes questioning, perspective.*

## 3.4    What is the trust's role (or purpose)?

An employee trust's core purpose will be to benefit its employees. Employee benefit can be both *financial* and *non-financial*.

### (a)  Financial benefits

### *(i)  Bonus or profit share*

The most likely financial benefit for employees will (subject of course to their company's performance) be a *bonus* or *profit share*. This will generally be the key employee benefit, apart from in companies that are *not-for-profit* and whose overriding purpose is the provision of a particular public service (for example, many social enterprises and Community Interest Companies (CICs)).

Where an employee trust acquires shares in an existing company, a period of time will commonly have to pass before it is possible to pay bonuses that are substantially larger than those paid previously.

This is because the trust will have agreed with the selling shareholders to pay for their shares,  the purchase price being paid over a period of years after the trust's purchase, funded by contributions to the trust from the company's annual profits (for further information, please see Chapter 7). In the early years of the company becoming employee-owned this will place significant demands on the company's profits, limiting any scope for profit sharing with employees. As purchase price instalments are paid off, however, a higher proportion of profits will be available to be shared with employees.

In practice, though, employees will quite reasonably be expecting to see a tangible benefit from employee ownership in the early years. It is therefore recommended that a new, or revised, bonus arrangement be put in place which (conditional on a strong enough profit performance by the company) will enable employees to enjoy a new financial reward linked to performance, albeit initially this may be at a relatively modest level.

Where the trust is an employee ownership trust, a bonus can be paid to each employee free of income tax. For a company that already operated a company-wide bonus scheme before the employee ownership trust acquired control, this facility can enable employees to receive an increased net reward without any additional cost to the company.

### (ii)    Capital growth

The other kind of financial benefit for employees is *capital growth*, but this may not always be desired and, if it is to be an objective, will need careful planning.

Capital growth means the ability to share in any growth in the company's value through improved profit over a period of time. There are two ways in which employees could enjoy this benefit in a company which is majority owned by an employee trust:

- *the trustees could, after a period of growth, sell the trust's shares to a third-party buyer. After payment of any taxes and expenses of sale, the net proceeds would (assuming this is what the trust deed provides for) be shared between the employees;*

*or*

- *the trustees could transfer some of the trust's shares to individual employees. These shares would be retained for a period of time (for example, until the employee left the company and was then required to sell them, or until they wished to sell voluntarily), after which the trust would buy them back.*

Each of these approaches raises important issues.

It would be major step for the trustees to sell the trust's entire holding to a third party, since the company would then no longer be employee-owned. The trustees would need to consider very carefully the relative advantages and disadvantages for employees as beneficiaries of the trust.

If the trustees were instead to transfer some of the trust's shares to individual employees, the company's employee ownership structure would become more complex. Also, to ensure that individual employee shareholders were ultimately able to turn their shares into cash, it is likely that the company would need to divert some of its profits to the trust to ensure it had the funds to pay the purchase price to selling employees.

### (b) Non-financial benefits
Employees will also have non-financial interests. For example, trustees of an employee trust will often consider that it is in the interests of employees for:
- *their work to have a clear and positive purpose, with job satisfaction and fulfilment*
- *any ethos, vision and/or values of the company to be pursued*
- *there to be opportunities for career progression*
- *them to be engaged in the company's success*
- *the company's leadership culture to be listening and participative*
- *the company to have a commitment to the community in which it operates.*

Achievement of these goals is more likely than not to have a positive impact on the company's performance, so in a successful employee-owned company there will be a strong link between non-financial and financial benefits.

What is the trustees' role in the delivery of these non-financial benefits? As the company's controlling shareholders, the trustees will be in a position to require the directors to lead the company in a way which maximises the likelihood of these aims being achieved. So, a key part of the trustees' role will often be to listen to the employees' views as to how effectively non-financial interests are pursued, identify any areas for improvement and then raise these with the company's directors.

## 3.5    Legal duties of trustees

In legal parlance, an employee trust is known as a *discretionary trust*. This means that the trustees have wide scope to decide how to confer benefit on beneficiaries, although this scope is considerably narrowed for the trustees of an employee ownership trust (see Chapter 6).

The main other kind of trust that may be encountered as part of a company's ownership is a *bare trust*. This is different in nature from an employee trust.

With a bare trust, the trustees hold property on behalf of a named individual on terms that the individual has full powers to direct how that property should be used for his or her benefit. Where that property is shares, the individual's powers would often include a requirement to pay income from the shares (dividends) over to him or her, to exercise voting rights according to the individual's wishes and to sell the shares and transfer the sale proceeds to him or her. In reality, the individual has all the ownership rights of those shares, but to the outside world the trustees are shown as the owners.

With an employee trust, in general no particular individual has personal ownership rights over any of the trust's shares or other assets. The trustees hold the assets on behalf of a group of beneficiaries, with full discretion as to how they may be used as a benefit and for whom. It is possible, however, for the trustees to allocate particular assets to a particular beneficiary, the effect of which is that they would have created a separate bare trust for that person, underneath the main employee trust.

Bare trusts are sometimes used in an employee-owned company. If shares in an employee-owned company are to be transferred from an employee trust to individual employees, this is sometimes done through a tax advantaged arrangement called a Share Incentive

Plan (SIP). Under a SIP, shares are allocated to individual employees and then held on their behalf in a special SIP trust, which is a modified form of bare trust. Chapter 10 contains further information about SIPs.

A discretionary trust is fundamentally different from a bare trust. No individual has personal ownership rights over specific shares. Instead, the trustees have power to decide how employees should benefit and are not obliged (so long as the trust is not an employee ownership trust) necessarily to confer benefit on all employees.

### (a) The general legal duties of the trustees of an employee trust
The general duties of the trustees of an employee trust may be summarised as follows:
- as we have considered, the trustees have a general duty to act in the best interests of the beneficiaries
- trustees must not act with improper motives
- nothing trustees do must be fraudulent
- trustees must not act dishonestly or in bad faith
- trustees must consider the relevant facts and take into account relevant matters
- trustees must not confer any benefit on any person who is not a beneficiary
- trustees must not act capriciously
- trustee decisions must be objectively reasonable
- trustees are under no duty to consult with beneficiaries or to follow their wishes.

Trustees are human and may sometimes make decisions that others would not. So long as they comply with their duties as set out above, and in particular ensure that their decisions can objectively be considered as reasonable, they will have discharged their duty.

### (b) What are the duties of trustees in practice?
The trustees of an employee trust holding a majority of shares in a company effectively control the ownership of that company. A principal duty will be to monitor the performance of the company and ensure that its directors are running it in the best interests of the beneficiaries as a whole. Without a financially successful business, there can be no paid employment, so clearly a priority for

the trustees will be to ensure that at the very least the business is solvent and can pay its debts. Of course, most employee-owned companies have the goal of making profits that can be shared with their shareholders and, often, to see these profits grow over time, increasing the financial reward to employees.

Some employee-owned companies do not place as much importance on profit, prioritising the achievement of a particular social purpose. But they will still be subject to financial disciplines and the trustees will wish to ensure that these are being adhered to.

The trust deed will typically set out some specific duties on the trustees which relate to that particular employee trust and may also contain some additional provisions which are intended to ensure that the trustees focus on fostering a participative management style in the company.

In practice, the trustees should normally be consulted by the company's directors on all major decisions, including annual budget and target setting and business planning, and the trustees will hold regular meetings with the company's directors to review performance.

Should the trustees of an employee trust holding a majority of a company's shares ever be unhappy with the performance of the company's directors, they have – like any controlling shareholder – a statutory right under company law to replace any of the directors.

Acting as a trustee is an important role, and it is strongly recommended that trustees obtain training in how to perform their role as effectively as possible.

### (c)  Do the trustees manage the Company?
The trustees' role is not to *manage the company*. That is the job of the company's *directors* (please see below).

### 3.6    The role of the company's directors
The *directors of the company* will play a very different role from that played by the *trustees of an employee trust*. The directors' primary job is to provide leadership in the company, ensuring that it is profitable and planning ahead as necessary. As mentioned above,

the trustees will wish to see that the company continues to be managed in ways that maximise employee engagement and the directors will be expected to take account of that.

Under the Companies Act 2006, directors' duties also include the following:

- to act within their powers
- to promote the Company's success, taking the following into account:
  - the likely consequences of any decision in the long term
  - the interests of the company's employees
  - the need to foster the company's business relationships with suppliers, customers and others
  - the impact of the company's operations on the community and the environment
  - the desirability of the company maintaining a reputation for high standards of business conduct
  - the need to act fairly as between the members of the company.
- to exercise independent judgement
- to exercise reasonable skill, care and diligence
- to avoid conflicts of interest
- not to accept benefits from third parties
- to declare any personal interests in a proposed transaction or arrangement with the company.

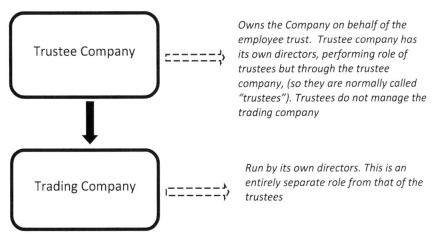

Trustee Company

Owns the Company on behalf of the employee trust. Trustee company has its own directors, performing role of trustees but through the trustee company, (so they are normally called "trustees"). Trustees do not manage the trading company

Trading Company

Run by its own directors. This is an entirely separate role from that of the trustees

**To recap:**

- Every trust will be run by its trustees (or directors of a specially formed trustee company – where this is the case they are often still called trustees).
- An employee trust's role is to benefit the company's employees (*beneficiaries*).
- Benefit can be financial (bonus/profit share, and sometimes capital growth) and non-financial (e.g. better working conditions).
- Trustees have certain legal duties and the trust deed will normally contain its own requirements.
- The trustees do not manage the company, but they will have a duty to do what they reasonably can to ensure the company is well managed.
- The company's directors who are responsible for managing the company. They also have their own set of legal duties.

# 4   Setting up an employee trust: key steps and decisions

## 4.1   What stage are you at?

The amount of planning that will be required will partly depend on whether you are setting up an employee trust to be the owner of a new or recently established company or to acquire a company from existing shareholders as part of an ownership succession plan. The latter is likely to involve more steps than the former because, in addition to considering how the trust will to be structured, it will also be necessary to determine the terms of its share purchase, what the shares are worth and how the purchase price is going to be funded.

As you will need to think about how the trust and its ownership of the company will be structured in either of these situations, we will start with that.

## 4.2   What kind of employee trust?

As we have seen in Chapter 3, there are two main kinds of employee trust: the *employee benefit trust* and the *employee ownership trust*. We have also mentioned the *bare trust* but this is unlikely to play any significant role in the ownership of most employee-owned companies.

An employee benefit trust and an employee ownership trust can each be at the core  of an employee-owned company's ownership, but they have relative advantages and disadvantages. The table below summarises these:

|  | Advantages | Disadvantages |
|---|---|---|
| Employee benefit trust (EBT) | Trustees have wide discretion as to how to confer benefit on beneficiaries, giving wider flexibility (where this is an objective) Holders of 5% or more of the company's shares can benefit from the trust if they | Sellers to an employee benefit trust pay CGT No ability for the company to pay employees income tax free bonuses For a company wishing to formalise ownership by all its employees, an EBT is unlikely to be appropriate as its wide |

| | pay income tax on what they receive | discretionary nature allows benefit to be skewed to certain employees only |
|---|---|---|
| Employee ownership trust (EOT) | Sellers of a controlling interest in their company to an EOT can claim exemption from CGT<br>Employees of a company in which an EOT has a controlling interest can receive income tax free bonuses<br>An EOT is a recognised all-employee ownership structure | Where employees receive any benefit from the EOT (for example if it offers them the opportunity to acquire shares), this must be on the same terms as for all other employees (but some companies will consider that an advantage as it shows a clear commitment to widespread employee ownership)<br>Holders of 5% or more of the company's shares cannot benefit from the trust |

In evaluating the tax reliefs associated with employee ownership trusts, it will be important to have a full understanding of the various conditions. These are considered in Chapter 6.

## 4.3   Will there be other shareholders?

Will the company be 100% owned by an employee trust or will there also be other shareholders?  More specifically:

- *If the trust is purchasing shares from existing shareholders, are they selling the entire company or retaining some shares?*
- *Will an investor purchase new shares in the company to provide new funding?*
- *Is it intended that the trust transfer some of its shares to employees over time, so that the company's employee ownership will be a hybrid of trust and individual share ownership?*
- *Will directors or other members of the company's senior leadership team have the opportunity to invest or be rewarded in shares, to a greater extent than employees generally?[7]*

---

[7] If the trust is an employee ownership trust, the *same terms* rule will prevent it from transferring shares to selected employees. However, it would be permissible for the company to issue new shares to selected

## (a) Hybrid employee ownership?

The table which follows compares employee ownership which is purely through an employee trust and a hybrid arrangement under which employee trust ownership is combined with personal employee share ownership (for example the trust holds 80% and employees hold 20% of the shares). The table's aim is to indicate which may be more appropriate depending on the company's objectives in becoming employee-owned and also its particular circumstances. Under each stated objective or circumstance, there follows a short italicised explanatory note.

| Trust retains all shares indefinitely (indirect (trust) ownership) | Trust retains some shares permanently but distributes some to employees (hybrid ownership) |
|---|---|
| **Capital growth for employees not an objective** Where an annual bonus or profit share (depending on performance) is considered sufficient financial reward and/or there is limited scope for the business to grow in value | **Capital growth important for employees** So they can acquire shares and sell them at a gain in the future as company value grows because of improved performance |
| **Higher staff turnover** This would increase the administration involved in issuing shares and buying them back from departing employees (or other employees wishing to sell) | **Low staff turnover** Because the lower the frequency of employees leaving and new staff joining, the lower the administration involved in issuing shares and buying them back |
| **Larger employee numbers** As above: also increases the administration involved in personal share ownership | Smaller employee numbers As above: smaller employee numbers reduce the administration involved in |

employees. This would reduce the trust's percentage holding but would not involve it transferring any of its own shares to any employees.

| | |
|---|---|
| **Long term employee ownership is important**<br>Significant levels of personal share ownership could eventually create pressure for the company to be sold, to allow employees to realise the full value of the shares in which they have personally invested | personal share ownership<br>Employees likely to consider personal share ownership more real than trust ownership<br>For example, where a company has financially motivated/aware employees who will place a high value on owning their own shares<br>Tax breaks for individual share ownership make it more attractive and affordable<br>The SIP[8] and potentially other statutory tax advantaged arrangements provide significant tax incentives for employees acquiring shares personally<br>Income tax free dividends of up to £2000 per employee can be paid each year |
| **Desire to prevent (or make difficult) a takeover**<br>If this is a goal, trustees could agree to sell the company only if they thought that was in the beneficiaries' best interests, whereas individual shareholders only have their own personal interests to take into account | |
| **Employees may have difficulty funding share acquisition**<br>This is a very common challenge. Sometimes it is addressed by the company lending employees money to fund their share purchase | |

---

[8] Under a SIP (Share Incentive Plan) employees can:
- purchase shares by salary deduction and be given income tax relief on the purchase price; and/or
- be awarded free shares without being subject to income tax on their value as a benefit in kind.

(See Chapter 10 for further information)

| Limited funds to buy back employees' shares | |
|---|---|
| The greater the percentage of the company held by employees, the greater the longer term financial cost to the company of buying their shares back. In a successful and growing company, this total cost will grow and new employees are unlikely to be able to afford to buy out employees who are selling. Such a company may risk being a victim of its own success<br><br>If bonuses / performance-based rewards are important, the company is happy for these to be cash-based rather than involving shares<br><br>Where the trust is an employee ownership trust which controls the company, income tax free bonuses may be an added attraction | |
| **Desire to keep ownership as simple as possible** | |
| Leaving all shares in an employee trust is simpler than combining trust and individual share ownership | |

## (b) Separate share ownership arrangements for members of the company's senior leadership team?

It is going to be important to ensure that the company's directors, other senior leaders and key employees are effectively rewarded. If a profit share or performance related bonus is considered important, one can be introduced. The requirement that bonuses be paid to all employees on the same terms applies only to income tax free bonuses in a company that is majority-owned by an employee ownership trust, and there is nothing to prevent any employee-owned company establishing a bonus or profit share plan for its key employees only.

Alternatively, or in some cases additionally, some companies take the view that selected senior staff should have the opportunity to acquire a personal share ownership stake alongside the majority stake held by an employee trust (and in a hybrid arrangement, also alongside the personal shareholdings held by other employees).

Where this is done, the number of shares which can be acquired by a senior employee will typically be greater than the maximum number that a non-senior staff member may hold. If the company is majority owned by an employee ownership trust, the same terms rule will prevent this trust from being the source of shares for senior staff members. Instead, the shares will need to be new shares issued by the company or, if there are other shareholders apart from the employee ownership trust and non-senior employees (for example, the former majority owners who have retained a minority holding) they could supply shares for senior staff.

If this kind of personal share ownership is favoured, it is also recommended to consider how the shares are to be delivered. Chapters 5 and 12-14 consider this further.

## 4.4   What is the current legal structure of the business?

A business can be owned and operated by a limited company, a partnership, a limited liability partnership (LLP) or by a single person (sole trader).

The vast majority of UK businesses are operated by limited companies, and this structure is most compatible with employee ownership. Whilst it may be possible to introduce some degree of employee ownership into a partnership or LLP, it is likely to be more complex.

The tax advantages of an employee ownership trust are available only where it owns a majority of shares in a company.

The message from this is that if your business is not run through a company and you want to access the tax advantages that come with being majority owned by an employee ownership trust, you will have to transfer your business to a company. Also, if you want to create any other form of employee ownership this is probably going to be far easier if a company owns your business.

## 4.5 Who will the trustees be?

This question primarily considers what kinds of individual should be appointed as trustees. However, before looking at that, we should first consider whether the trustees are to perform this role directly or through a specially formed company (a *trustee company* or *corporate trustee*).

### (a) Individual trustees or a trustee company?

Acting as a trustee brings significant responsibilities and a trustee who fails in their duties or contravenes the terms of the trust can face personal liability for any resulting financial loss to beneficiaries. Whilst this risk can be addressed by taking out insurance and by exercising due skill and care, trustees can be further sheltered from personal liability if they perform their role by acting as directors of a trustee company, which gives them additional protection through limited liability.

Unless there are particular reasons favouring trustees acting individually, it is normally recommended to use a trustee company. That company would be appointed as the single trustee of the trust, and its directors would be the individuals performing the trustee role.

So, in effect, the "trustees" of the trust would be the individuals who have been appointed as directors of the trustee company. This is an entirely different role from being a director of the company operating the business.

### (b) Where will the trust be resident?

An employee trust can be based (resident) in the UK or overseas.

There is a potential tax advantage in establishing an employee trust offshore, which is that (depending on the location) it will not be subject to taxation on any gains it makes should it sell its shares in the future (see Chapter 6), whereas if resident in the United Kingdom its gains will be subject to CGT.

But taxation is not the only consideration. If an employee trust has an offshore trustee, it is very likely that this will be a professional trustee company whose employees administer a large number of other trusts for other clients and who may not be accustomed to running a trust which owns an entire business. For a company which has an employee trust as its principal or only shareholder, it is important that the trustees are engaged in the company's business, visible and accessible to employees on a regular basis and that they have a strong working relationship with the company's senior leadership team. In most cases, it will be preferable to have UK-based trustees for whom these goals will be more straightforward to achieve than would be the case if they were more remotely located.

### (c) Who should be the trustees?

Unless a single professional trustee company is appointed, you will need to consider what kinds of individual should be the trustees. There are no rules, other than a requirement to have a minimum of two trustees where the trustees are individuals and no trustee company is involved.

This is covered further in Chapter 3, under *Who runs the trust?*

## 4.6 Who will be the beneficiaries?

Who can or should be a beneficiary will depend on whether the trust is an employee benefit trust or an employee ownership trust.

### (a) Employee benefit trust

Beneficiaries can be broadly defined under an employee benefit trust. However, to ensure that the trust is to avoid a number of tax traps, it is the beneficiaries will generally defined by reference to their employment with the company which is creating the trust. Subject to that, there is considerable scope to include dependants of employees as beneficiaries and to set a qualifying period of employment before an individual can be included as a beneficiary.

### (b) Employee ownership trust

#### (i) *If the trust is an employee ownership trust, the rules are tighter:*

- *All employees must be beneficiaries (although it is possible to stipulate a qualifying period of employment of up to twelve months).*
- *Directors and officers can be beneficiaries although they are not employees (but they do not have to be).*
- *Dependants of a deceased employee can be beneficiaries (but do not have to be) for a year following death.*

- *Individuals holding at least 5% of shares in the company (including persons connected with them) may not be beneficiaries.*

Chapter 6 contains more detailed information on these requirements.

## 4.7    How will the trustees make decisions?

Here there are two main issues to consider:

- How many trustees need to be present at a trustee meeting?
- What percentage of trustees need to support a particular decision for it to be effective?

### (a)  How many trustees need to be present for a trustee meeting to go ahead?

This is what is called the *quorum requirement*. A trustee meeting may only proceed if the required number or percentage of trustees is present.

This could be specified as a minimum number or as a percentage of trustees.

Where the trustees are drawn from different categories (for example, trustees who are employees or trustees who are former shareholders) it might be specified in the trust deed that a quorum is only present if a trustee from a specified category is present.

### (b)  What percentage of trustees need to support a particular decision for it to be effective?

Trust law says that trustee decisions must be unanimous, unless the trust deed provides otherwise. Where a trust has a single corporate trustee (so the trustee decisions are made by that company's directors) this rule does not apply, which means decisions can be made by majority vote.

So if an employee trust is to have individual trustees, the default position is that only decisions made unanimously will be valid. If it considered more appropriate for trustees to decide by majority vote, this is permitted, as long as it is provided for in the trust deed.

If the trust has a corporate trustee, majority vote is the default position, so if unanimity is preferred that will need to be stipulated in the trust deed.

In practice, it is recommended that the trust deed always covers this question. It does not need to be a binary choice between majority or unanimous vote. It is possible for a trust deed to allow for majority vote generally but for particular matters to require unanimity (for example a decision to sell the company).

**To recap:**
Some key things to consider If you are setting up an employee trust:
- Should it be an employee ownership trust or an employee benefit trust?
- Will existing shareholders retain any of their shares?
- Will employees or directors acquire any shares personally?
- Is the business already operated by a company? If not (e.g. a limited liability partnership) it may need to convert to a company (and must do if the tax reliefs associated with an employee ownership trust are to be claimed).
- Who are going to be the trustees?
- Who are going to be the beneficiaries (e.g. do you want to stipulate a period of employment before an employee qualifies as a beneficiary)?
- How are the trustees going to make decisions?

# 5 Individual employee share ownership

## 5.1 When might a company be individually employee-owned?

As has been explored in Chapter 2, there are a number of reasons why many employee-owned companies choose an ownership structure in which an employee trust holds all, or a majority, of the shares.

The main challenges created by *individual share ownership* are set out below:

| *Administration* | A reliable system will be needed which enables new employees to acquire shares and (in many cases) requires or enables departing employees to sell. This can be intricate and resource heavy. The larger the company the more substantial the task, and a company with high staff turnover is also likely to find this creates a lot of work |
|---|---|
| *Enabling employees to buy* | Employees rarely have sufficient funds to invest in their company. This can, however, be mitigated by using options to defer the purchase price or by using a tax advantaged employee share plan such as the SIP |
| *Enabling employees to sell* | Eventually, employees will wish to sell their shares. If there are not sufficient new buyers, the company will need to consider funding the purchase, which can place a burden on long term cash flow, particularly where the shares have significantly grown in value |

That does not mean there is no place for the direct holding of shares by individual employees. There are circumstances where this will be appropriate, falling into these main categories:

| | |
|---|---|
| *Hybrid (see Chapter 2)* | Whilst the majority of the company is owned by an employee trust, there is also scope for individual employees to hold shares personally |
| *Co-operative* | Historically co-operatives have involved 100% of their shares being owned directly by employees,[9] for example Suma Wholefoods and the Spanish manufacturing group, Mondragon |
| *Others* | Other individually employee-owned companies exist, many of which are consultancy businesses |

This chapter considers ways in which employees can purchase shares personally.

## 5.2 How an employee can personally acquire shares in their company

The employee share ownership world is replete with jargon which may give the impression you are about to enter a disorientating labyrinth:

- buying shares
- being given shares
- being granted a right to acquire shares (by buying or being given them) at some point in the future (or even straight away): this is known as a share option.

Each of these is considered in turn.

### (a) Buying shares

Here, an employee will buy shares (either from existing shareholders or by the company issuing new shares to them), paying either their market value or a discounted price.

Clearly, the employee will need to fund the purchase price, and often they will not easily be able to do so.

---

[9] For further reading about co-operatives, we recommend the Co-ops UK website www.uk.coop/uk and their book, *Simply Legal*

If the purchase price is discounted below market value, the employee will also be subject to income tax (and possibly also National Insurance, depending on the circumstances) on the discount, as this is regarded as employment income.[10]

Any income tax will be paid by the employee under self-assessment unless the same circumstances that create a National Insurance liability also apply, in which case both the income tax and the primary (employee's) National Insurance will be paid by the company under PAYE and then recovered from the employee.

Later in this chapter ways to make it easier financially for employees to purchase shares are considered.

### (b) Being given shares

The general rule under UK tax legislation is that the value of free shares received by an employee is regarded as part of their employment income so is subject to income tax (and potentially also National Insurance – see 5.2(a) above).

There is a limited number of ways in which this tax liability can legitimately be mitigated.

### (c) Share options

An employee can be granted an option to acquire shares at or from a later date. The principal attraction of a share option from the company's perspective is that it creates an incentive for the employee to stay with the company and perform effectively. If the employee leaves before they have acquired the right to turn their option into actual shares (*exercise the option*) they might lose it, or may lose part of it, depending on the reason they left and/or when they leave. If the company's profits grow over the lifetime of the option then generally its value will grow. Since the option allows

---

[10] The main (but not only situation) when National Insurance, both employee (primary) and employer (secondary), will be due is if the shares acquired by the employee can be turned into cash. This would be the case in a listed company and also in some private companies if there is, for example, a market in the shares. In these situations, the employee's income tax would be collected under PAYE rather than self-assessment. See Chapter 14.2 for further information.

the employee to buy shares at a fixed price, the value of the option grows in line with the growth in value of the company's shares.

Granting an employee an option can more attractive for them financially compared with inviting them to buy, or giving them, shares. If the option exercise price is nil (so the shares will effectively be free), no tax liability arises until the option is exercised. If the exercise price is set at a higher level (for example, market value when the option is granted) there will be the same tax timing advantage and it will only be necessary for the employee to pay the exercise price when the option is exercised.

*(i)  What should be the terms of a share option?*
Set out in the table which follows is a summary of fundamental points to consider when structuring an option:

| Term of option | Comment |
|---|---|
| *What should the option exercise price be (the price which the employee must pay if they want to exercise their option and buy the shares)?* | The option exercise price can be set at any level. Most commonly it will be equal to the market value of the shares under option on the date when the option is granted. It could also be set below market value on the date of grant or (unusually) above market value |
| *When can the option be exercised?* | This is often after a period of time (maybe a year or more) has elapsed, or the option might become exercisable in time-based instalments (this is called vesting) Where a company's shareholders plan to grow the company and then seek a buyer (less common in an employee-owned company), the right to exercise the option may be linked to a buyer being found |
| *What happens if the optionholder (employee) leaves?* | If they leave before the option has become exercisable, the option may "lapse" If the option lapses it effectively ceases to exist and the optionholder will not have any further rights to acquire the shares under option. Some options however provide that if the employee leaves, in certain circumstances, they will be allowed to retain their vested options for later exercise or to exercise them within a limited period of leaving |

| | |
|---|---|
| *Should there be a separate performance target?* | As the value of options is directly linked to the growth in value of the company, options have an intrinsic performance target. But some companies also wish to require achievement of a specific performance target as a condition of the option becoming capable of exercise |
| *What is the tax treatment?* | This will depend on the circumstances<br>Under an "unapproved" or "non-approved" option, which would be one granted without using one of the available tax advantaged arrangements, the employee will be subject to income tax when they exercise the option, on the difference between the price paid (exercise price) and the value of the shares on the date of exercise. National Insurance will also be due if the shares are then readily convertible into cash and in some other circumstances (see Chapter 14)<br>If the option is granted as an EMI or CSOP option (see Chapters 12 and 13) with an exercise price not less than market value on the date when the option was granted, no tax will be due until the shares are eventually sold. At that point, the optionholder's gains will be subject to CGT |

## 5.3    How to mitigate the financial cost for employees

In this part we review the different ways in which any financial cost to employees of acquiring shares in their company can be mitigated or removed.

## (a)  Buying shares

### (i)  *Income tax relief on the purchase price*

Under the *Share Incentive Plan (SIP)* a company's employees can be invited to purchase shares, paid for by a regular deduction from their salary. The money deducted is not subject to income tax or National Insurance. In other words, the SIP offers employees and company alike tax relief on the purchase price.

A key condition is that if an invitation to acquire shares is made under a SIP, that invitation must be offered to all the company's employees (or all employees who have completed a minimum period of continuous employment of no more than eighteen months).

There are other conditions. These are considered in more detail in Chapter 10.

Employees may be given an additional incentive to purchase shares by offering them free shares to match those purchased (up to two free matching shares for every one share purchased). We consider under Chapter 10 how free shares can be awarded under a SIP.

A SIP can be a suitable way for an employee ownership trust or an employee benefit trust to sell shares to individual employees. Participation is not compulsory so any employee who does not wish to purchase shares is automatically opted out if they do not take up the invitation.

### (ii) Paying for the shares later

It is possible for employees to defer the date when they must pay for their shares, if the company (or other seller, for example another shareholder) agrees to this. This arrangement is often called *nil paid shares*.

If the employee is not required to pay interest on the deferred amount, this will be treated as a taxable benefit for income tax purposes and they will be required to pay tax on the annual interest amount from which they have been released, at the HM Revenue and Customs official rate for "notional loans".

There will be no income tax liability if interest is paid at the same official rate (or a higher rate).

Acquiring shares which are to be paid for at a later date will be regarded as a "regulated activity" under the Financial Services and Markets Act 2000. Depending on the circumstances, the terms of the loan and the status of the employee, this may require the company to obtain authorisation from the Financial Conduct Authority and may also require certain procedures to be followed and documents to be supplied to the employee. This is considered in more detail in Chapter 16.

A vital aspect, about which company and employee alike must be made very clear, is that once nil paid shares have been acquired they must eventually be paid for. If the company becomes insolvent and it has any nil paid shares not yet paid for, their holders should expect to receive a demand to pay for them. Nil paid shares should always come with a prominent health warning and are not recommended other than for employees who fully understand the conditions which attach to them.

An offer of nil paid shares can be made to any employees selected by the company.

### (iii) Growth shares

A third potential approach is for a company to create a new class of shares which will only entitle their holders to a stake in the company's value when that value exceeds a certain level. These are called *growth shares*.

For example, a company which has a value of £1.5 million might create a class of growth shares under which each employee acquiring them will share in a specified percentage of growth in value above £1.7 million if their shares are ever sold or the company is liquidated.

HM Revenue and Custom's current practice is to accept that when those shares are first acquired they will have a low value because if the company were sold at that time they would not entitle their holder to any part of the sale proceeds. This means that the purchase price can be kept at a correspondingly low level without a tax liability arising on any discount.

Growth shares have some disadvantages. If, in the above example, a further award of the same class of growth share was to be made at a time when the company's value had grown to £2 million, those shares would then have material value because the £1.7 million threshold would have been reached. To avoid this, it would be necessary to have a second class of growth shares with a higher value threshold. Without careful advance planning, the company's articles of association would need to be changed each time to achieve this.

Growth shares are more complex to explain to employees than many of the alternatives.

An offer of growth shares can be made to any employees selected by the company.

Whilst there may be occasions when they are suitable in an employee-owned company, it is likely that these will be rare and limited to situations where senior leaders are to acquire shares personally and there is no better alternative.

**(b) Free shares**

*(i) Free share awards under a SIP*
As well as providing tax relief on the purchase price of shares, a SIP also enables employees to be awarded free shares free of income tax and National Insurance.

Awards of free shares must be made to all employees who have sufficient qualifying employment (which is the same as for shares purchased under a SIP) although no employee is obliged to accept an award. Any offer of free shares must be made to each employee on the same terms.[11]

The tax reliefs are conditional on the employee remaining employed by that company for five years (unless they leave for certain specified reasons). If by leaving they lose the tax relief, they will have to pay income tax and National Insurance after all (and their employer company will have to pay employer's National Insurance). Other conditions for free share awards are considered in more detail in Chapter 10.

Where it is desired, in a company majority-owned by an employee ownership trust or an employee benefit trust, to give shares to individual employees, free shares under a SIP should be given careful consideration. Participation is not compulsory so any

---

[11] This means either all employees are offered the same number of free shares, or varying amounts depending on their salary, length of service or hours worked (or a combination of those factors).

employee who does not wish to purchase shares is automatically opted out if they do not take up the invitation.

Under a SIP, employees can be offered free shares in these main ways:
- free shares alone (not matched to the purchase of shares)
- both free shares and share purchase (see above)
- share purchase and free matching shares
- free shares, share purchase and free matching shares.

*(ii)  Granting an employee the right to acquire free shares at a later date*

In effect, this means granting an employee an option to acquire shares at or from a later date, perhaps subject to a performance condition being achieved.

This defers any tax liability until the option is exercised or, for certain kinds of option, until the employee has sold the shares. For the employee it brings the significant advantage that they will have a choice between:
- exercising the option and acquiring the shares, incurring a tax liability either then or on eventually selling the shares; or
- if they do not wish to incur a tax liability, they can choose not to exercise the option, or only to do so when they are ready to pay the tax.

The employee will have the comfort of knowing that their option gives them the right to acquire shares (subject to any conditions in their option agreement) and they can decide whether they wish to take it up.

Because of the requirement that if an employee ownership trust is to transfer shares it must to transfer to all employees who have reached a qualifying period of employment, options by their very nature are not appropriate for such transfers. Although a grant of options could be made to all employees (and on the same terms), it is unlikely that all will be exercised. For example, employees may leave and their options lapse, which would mean the "all-employee" requirement not being satisfied.

However, an employee benefit trust can grant options, as can the company itself, by agreeing to issue new shares when options are exercised. In the latter case, company law will mean that the option exercise price cannot be set at nil. The minimum exercise price per share must be equal to that share's nominal value.

Deferring the time when an employee acquires free shares is not the only advantage of a share option. For example, the share acquisition price under a share option can be set at a level (i.e. market value when the option is granted) which means they are not a deferred gift.

The next part looks at how the financial cost to employees to whom options are granted can be mitigated.

### (c) Share options

As we have seen in Chapter 5, the starting point for the taxation of share options granted to an employee is that the employee will pay income tax, and possibly also National Insurance, if they exercise their option, on the difference between the exercise price and the shares' value at the date of exercise.

An employee holding options over shares in a listed company may be able to sell sufficient shares to pay the tax liability, whereas if the option is over private company shares this may be more difficult or even impossible.

There are three possible ways of structuring options in a way that:
- defers any tax liability beyond the date of option exercise to the date when the shares are eventually sold; and
- results in the employee paying CGT rather than income tax and possibly also National Insurance.

We consider each in turn.

### (i) EMI options

Under EMI (Enterprise Management Incentive) options, any growth in value of shares between option grant and eventual sale is subject to CGT. Under current rates, this means a rate of either 10% or 20% depending on the circumstances.[12]

For a company which believes options are the right way for its key employees to become shareholders, it is recommended that EMI options be considered first. Compared with the two other kinds of tax advantaged options considered later in this chapter, it has these main advantages:

- a relatively high financial limit
- a high degree of flexibility in its design
- the lowest potential tax rate.

As with all statutory tax advantaged employee share schemes, conditions have to be met before a company can grant EMI options. These are considered in more detail in Chapter 12 but are summarised here:

| Condition | How it works |
|---|---|
| Independent company | The company granting the options must not be controlled by another company (so EMI options cannot be granted over shares in a subsidiary) |
| Maximum size of company when the option is granted | The company's gross (total) assets must not be more than £30 million. *Please note this is different from net assets.* Also, it must not have more than 250 full-time (or full-time equivalent) employees |
| The company must be trading (or preparing to trade) and its trade must not be an excluded one | Companies which do not trade may not grant EMI options. Also, a trading company is excluded if its trade is on a list of specified trades which are not considered to merit the tax reliefs |
| Permanent establishment in the UK | The company must have a minimum degree of presence in the UK |
| Type of share | EMI options may only be granted over ordinary shares which are fully paid up |

---

[12] The CGT rate on shares is 10% for basic rate income taxpayers and 20% for higher rate income taxpayers. However, entrepreneurs' relief can reduce the 20% rate to 10% (see the case study)

| Only full-time employees | EMI options are for full-time employees only. This means the employee either:<br>• works at least 25 hours per week; or<br>• works at least 75% of their total working time for their employer company.<br>The company may choose which employees are to receive options |
|---|---|
| Individuals with large shareholdings excluded | An employee who already holds 30% or more of the company's shares may not be granted EMI options. Shareholdings of certain of the employee's relatives (principally: spouse, civil partner, parent, child, grandparent, grandchild) are included in this 30%. |
| Exercise price can be set at any level | The price at which the shares may be purchased can be set equal to the market value of the shares at the date of grant, below that market value or above it (although the latter is not common) |
| Option may be exercised at any time | There is no minimum option period, although the estate of a deceased EMI optionholder may not exercise the option more than twelve months after death and if any option is exercised more than ten years after its grant, gains will be subject to income tax and possibly National Insurance |
| Maximum value of shares | No employee may hold EMI options over shares worth more than £250,000 (measured at the date of option grant). The aggregate value of EMI options granted by a single company (also measured at the date of grant of each option) must not exceed £3 million. |

**EMI options case study: Howgill Energy Limited**

*Enabling senior managers to acquire shares when they cannot immediately fund the purchase price*

Howgill Energy Limited, a company specialising in renewable energy, is to become 100% owned by an employee ownership trust. The trustees believe that the senior leadership team, currently comprising three executive directors, should be given the opportunity to acquire shares so that if the company's profits grow those directors will be rewarded by growth in the value of those shares.

The three directors all have young families and very limited spare personal capital, so are unable to make an immediate personal investment.

### Granting EMI options

It is decided instead to grant them EMI share options. These can be exercised (turned into shares) after three years if the director is still with the company.

The total number of shares (i.e. for all three of the directors) under option is equal to 10% of the company.

The option exercise price is set at an amount per share equal to its current market value of £5 (using a facility to agree value offered by HM Revenue and Customs). This is based on the company having a value of £2 million. The company also puts in place a performance related bonus plan to fund the optionholders' eventual option exercise price.

The EMI option is granted a few weeks after the date when the employee ownership trust becomes the 100% shareholder.

### Exercising the options

Three years later, the company's profits have grown with the result that each share is now worth £8. Each director holding options decides it makes sense to exercise their option and pay £5 per share (using bonuses they have received).

The result is that the trust's holding has now reduced to 90%. However, it now owns 90% of a company worth £3.2 million, making its shareholding worth £2.88 million (compared with £2 million when it held 100%).

### What happens next

Longer term, it is recognised that the directors will eventually wish to sell their shares. To avoid having to put the entire company up for sale, a plan is created under which the company will build up a cash reserve over a period of years which it can then use to fund the cost of buying back each director's shares.

### Taxation

At the time of eventual sale, each share has a value of £25. Capital gains tax (CGT) is paid on the £20 per share gain at a rate of 20% (or 10% if the shares are eligible for entrepreneurs' relief*). Each optionholder can also claim an exemption from CGT on the first £12,000 of their gains if they haven't used it on other capital gains.

*Under current tax rules, entrepreneurs' relief can be claimed on the sale of shares acquired through EMI options if at least two years have passed between option grant and sale and during the whole period between those two events the optionholder is an employee or director.*

### (ii) CSOP options

For a company which favours options but which is not eligible to grant EMI options, CSOP (*Company Share Option Plan*) options may be available instead.

As with EMI options, growth in value of shares between option grant and eventual sale is subject to CGT. However, entrepreneurs' relief is only available to ensure a 10% rate if the shares comprise at least a 5% holding and at least one year has passed up to the sale date, during which the individual has held the shares (not just the options) and has been an employee or officer of the company.

Unlike EMI options, there is no maximum size of company or excluded trade. However, the limit on the value of CSOP options per employee is substantially lower, at £30,000.

This table summarises the main conditions for CSOP options:

| Condition | How it works |
|---|---|
| Independent company | The company granting the options must not be controlled by another company (so no CSOP options can be granted over shares in a subsidiary), unless the company is listed |
| Type of share | CSOP options may only be granted over ordinary shares which are fully paid up |
| Only employees and full-time directors | CSOP options can be granted to full-time or part-time employees. But they may only be granted to full-time directors (working at least 25 hours per week).<br>The company may choose which employees are to receive options |
| Individuals with large shareholdings excluded | As with EMI options, an employee who already holds 30% or more of the company's shares may not be granted CSOP options. Shares held by certain of the employee's relatives (principally: spouse, civil partner, parent, child, grandparent, grandchild) are included in this 30% |
| Exercise price must be at least market | This is different to EMI options, under which the exercise price can be less than market value at date |

| value at date option is granted | of option grant |
|---|---|
| Options may only be exercised after three years | If CSOP options are exercised sooner, option gains will normally be subject to income tax and possibly National Insurance. However, if an employee leaves as a "good leaver" or the company is taken over in certain ways, this can be avoided |
| Maximum value of shares | No employee may hold CSOP options over shares worth more than £30,000 (measured at the date of option grant) |

## (iii) Save As You Earn (SAYE) options

These are popular in listed companies but not commonly found in private companies, including employee-owned ones.

Key differences from CSOP options are:

- SAYE options must be offered to all employees, or all who have completed a qualifying period of employment which can be set at no more than five years; and
- an employee wishing to be granted SAYE options must agree to save a certain amount of money each month towards the option exercise price, over a three or five year period. At the end of that period, they can withdraw their savings and either use them to exercise their option or keep the money.

This table summarises the main conditions for SAYE options:

| Condition | How it works |
|---|---|
| Independent company | The company granting the options must not be controlled by another company (so no SAYE options can be granted over shares in a subsidiary), unless the company is listed |
| Type of share | SAYE options may only be granted over ordinary shares which are fully paid up. Additional rules apply where a company has more than one class of share |
| Only employees and full-time directors | SAYE options can be granted to full-time or part-time employees. But they may only be granted to full-time directors (working at least 25 hours per week). SAYE options must be offered to all qualifying employees on the same or similar terms. This |

| | includes allowing employees to be offered differing numbers of options according to their remuneration, length of service or hours worked |
|---|---|
| Exercise price may be discounted from market value by up to 20% | This is different to CSOP options, under which the exercise price cannot be less than market value at date of option grant |
| May only be exercised after savings period of three or five years | If SAYE options are exercised sooner, option gains will normally be subject to income tax and possibly National Insurance. However, if an employee leaves as a "good leaver" or the company is taken over in certain ways, this can be avoided |
| Maximum value of shares | No employee may hold SAYE options over shares worth more than £22,500 (if the employee agrees to save over a three year period) or £37,500 (for saving over a five year period). In each case these limits are to the value of shares at the date the option is granted |

**To recap:**

- There are pros and cons to individual share ownership.
- Employees can acquire shares in their company by buying them, being given them or being granted options to acquire them in the future.
- Awards of free shares to employees will generally be subject to income tax, as will the purchase of shares for less than their market value.
- However, the SIP (an all-employee share scheme) allows employees to receive free shares tax free, or to purchase shares with tax relief.
- If employees are to buy shares for a nominal price, doing this through offering them growth shares can minimise any tax liability.
- If options are granted, it is important to think carefully about the main terms of the option (e.g. when it can be exercised).
- The SAYE option scheme (also an all-employee scheme) enables employees to enjoy low tax growth on shares.

- EMI and CSOP options (under which selected employees may participate) also enable employees to enjoy low tax growth on shares.

# 6 Requirements for employee ownership trust tax reliefs

To recap, Chapter 2 explains that two principal tax reliefs are available:

- Exemption from CGT on selling a controlling interest in a company to an employee ownership trust; and
- The ability to pay income tax free bonuses to employees of a company controlled by an employee ownership trust.

This chapter considers the conditions in detail.

## 6.1 Conditions applying to both reliefs

The following conditions must be satisfied to claim the CGT relief or pay income tax free bonuses to employees:

- the all-employee benefit requirement
- the equality requirement (part of the all-employee benefit requirement)
- the controlling interest requirement
- the trading requirement.

The CGT relief conditions are contained in the Taxation of Chargeable Gains Act, Part 7 (sections 236H to 236U).

The conditions for payment of income tax free bonuses are contained in the Income Tax (Earnings & Pensions) Act 2003, Part 4 (sections 312A to 312I).

We look at each of these conditions in turn.

### (a) All-employee benefit requirement

The all-employee benefit requirement is met if the terms of the trust:

- Prohibit its property from being applied otherwise than for the benefit of all **eligible employees** of the company whose employees are the trust's beneficiaries (or all eligible employees of the company and its subsidiaries, if there is a group of companies, on the same terms (the **equality requirement**);

- Prohibit the trustees from creating a new trust or transferring the trust's property to another trust unless this is a transfer to another employee ownership trust – an **authorised transfer**;
- Prohibit loans to beneficiaries; and
- Prohibit any change to the trust which would cause it to fail to comply with any of the above requirements.

## (i) *Some key terms and their meanings*

| | |
|---|---|
| *Authorised transfer* | A transfer to another trust which would qualify as an employee ownership trust |
| *Eligible employee* | Any employee or officer of the company (or group). However, certain individuals (*excluded participators*) are not eligible employees and may not be beneficiaries of an employee ownership trust |
| *Excluded participator* | A participator (in the main, this means shareholder but it also includes others who have rights to become a shareholder) who holds, or is entitled to acquire, 5% or more of the company's share capital (or who would be entitled to 5% or more of the company's assets if it was wound up), if the company is a close company. It also includes: <br> • 5% participators in any other close company that has transferred money or made another property disposition to the same trust, if that transfer would have been a transfer of value had it not been excluded by Inheritance Tax Act 1984, either section 13 or 13A <br> • any person who has been such a 5% participator during the ten years ending with the date when the trust first acquired property <br> • anyone connected with any such person. A "connected person" is defined in TCGA 1992, section 286 |
| *Close company* | A company controlled by five or fewer participators |
| *Equality requirement* | Please see the following paragraph. |

## (b) Equality requirement

Under the equality requirement:

- The trust deed must stipulate that if trust assets (e.g. shares or cash) are to be distributed to employees, this distribution must meet the equality requirement (see below); and
- If bonuses paid by the company to employees are to qualify for income tax, they must also be paid according to the equality requirement.

The *equality requirement* is that any distribution of assets from the trust, or payment under a bonus scheme that qualifies for relief, must be for the benefit *of* all *eligible employees* of a company or group on the *same terms*.

### (i) Same terms

*Same terms* means all employees (or all employees who have completed a qualifying period of employment of no more than 12 months) either:
- get equal amounts or
- receive different amounts according to their:
  - *remuneration*
  - *length of service, or*
  - *hours worked*
- or a combination of the above.

**The same terms requirement: an example**

A company may apply the permitted factors separately but may not multiply them.

So a company may, for example, do the following:
- Determine a maximum amount of cash per employee
- Multiply half of that amount by a factor based on remuneration
- Multiply the other half by a factor based on length of service.
- Pay a bonus of the amount that is the sum of the two multiplications.

Alternatively, a company may:
- Allocate points per employee according to their remuneration bands, years of service and/or hours worked
- Pay a bonus to each employee according to their points.

But a company may not, for example:
- Determine a maximum payment per employee
- Multiply that amount by a factor based on remuneration
- Multiply the result again by a factor based on length of service

- Pay a bonus on the amount that results from the above.

The same also applies where the employee ownership trust itself distributes assets to beneficiaries.

### (ii) Payments to a deceased employee's family

An employee ownership trust can (but does not have to) provide that if an eligible employee dies, the trust may confer benefit on that individual's spouse, civil partner or dependants, within 12 months after the death, without this infringing the equality requirement. The maximum amount of benefit is equal to the amount which would have been paid to the deceased employee if they were still alive and employed.

It is also permissible to pay income tax free bonuses to the personal representatives of a deceased employee for up to 12 months after the death.

Companies which separately provide death in service insurance to their employees may feel that this removes the need to include dependants of deceased employees if the trust transfers property to beneficiaries or if income tax free bonuses are paid.

### (iii) Continuous service requirement

An employee ownership trust deed may, but does not have to, include a requirement for trust beneficiaries to have completed a minimum period of continuous employment. This may be set at up to 12 months. This is useful if it is desirable to ensure that benefit from the trust does not go to short term employees and is only received by those who have made a longer term commitment.

In the same way, employees with less than 12 months (or a shorter period) continuous service may be excluded from entitlement to receive an income tax free bonus.

### (iv) Payments to charity

The trust deed may (but does not have to) allow trustees of an employee ownership trust to pass trust property to charity on a distribution.

When designing an employee ownership trust, it is always advisable to think ahead to a possible future situation in which the trust comes to an end. In practice, this is most likely to happen if the trust sells all its shares to a third party purchaser. A view sometimes taken is that in those circumstances employees should not receive a windfall gain (and indeed the prospect of getting one might be seen as an incentive for them to lobby the trustees to accept a takeover offer), and that this possibility should be removed by saying that the trust's assets (proceeds of sale in this example) will go to charity.

An alternative view is that once an employee ownership trust has acquired the company, if the trustees subsequently feel it is in the beneficiaries' best interests for the company to be sold and for them to share in sale proceeds, the trust deed should not stand in the way.

A third approach is to provide that at the end of the trust's life, part of its net proceeds will go to beneficiaries and part to charity.

### (v)    All employees must receive some benefit
An employee ownership trust must not allow any of the trust's property to be applied in a manner where some eligible employees receive nothing, while others receive a payment.

However, the following exclusions are permitted:
- employees who do not meet any minimum continuous service requirement (see above)
- a person who requests in writing to be excluded
- office holders (directors or a company secretary) who are not employees.

There is a similar requirement for income tax free bonuses. It is not permitted for some eligible employees to receive nothing while others receive a bonus.

The two exceptions to this are:
- employees who are subject to a disciplinary process can be excluded (see box below)
- employees who do not meet any minimum continuous service requirement (see above) can be excluded.

**Income tax free bonuses: excluding employees on disciplinary grounds**

A bonus plan may qualify for the income tax relief if it excludes:

- a person who, within the 12 months ending with the award date, was found guilty of gross misconduct in disciplinary proceedings
- a person currently subject to disciplinary proceedings. In this case, the employee's bonus payment may be suspended until the proceedings have been completed, and withheld altogether if they are found to have committed gross misconduct
- a person found guilty of gross misconduct or who is summarily dismissed during the period between the bonus being awarded and it actually being paid.

### (vi) Bonus plan must not contain features which favour particular groups of employees

Bonuses may not be paid income tax free if operated in a way which is likely to confer benefits wholly or mainly on directors or higher paid employees, or particular groups of employees.

### (c) Controlling interest requirement

An employee ownership trust must control the company (or group) whose employees are the trust's beneficiaries.

There are five parts to this requirement, which are explained below. The legislation refers to the company (or in a group, its principal (i.e. holding) company) as "C".

In relation to the income tax relief on bonuses, C is the company that pays the bonuses (or if that company is the member of a group, C is the principal company of the group.

### (i) The employee ownership trust must hold more than 50% of C's ordinary share capital

More than 50% of C's ordinary share capital of C must be held by the trust.

Ordinary share capital means all the issued share capital (by whatever name called) of C, other than capital in respect of which the holders have a right to a fixed rate dividend and no other right to share in the profits of the company.

## (ii)  Majority of the voting rights

The employee ownership trust must hold a majority of the voting rights in C.

## (iii)  The trust must be entitled to more than 50% of the profits

The trust must hold shares entitling it to more than 50% of the profits of C available for distribution.

The trust will be treated as being entitled to dividends even if the trustee waives its entitlement (which the trust deed will commonly require).

## (iv)  Trust must be entitled to more than 50% of C's assets on a winding up

If C were ever to be wound up, the trust must be entitled to more than 50% of the assets available to *equity holders* on a winding up.

*Equity holder* Essentially, equity holders are shareholders and loan creditors other than holders of "restricted preference shares" (as defined in CTA 2010, sections 160 and 161) and lenders who have made normal commercial loans.

HM Revenue and Customs have confirmed that, where an employee ownership trust has acquired control of a company and the company has guaranteed to the sellers that the trust will pay purchase price instalments on time, those sellers will not normally be regarded as equity holders simply by virtue of their entitlement to guaranteed payments.

## (v)  The Trustee's consent is needed for any reduction in its entitlement

There must be no provision in any agreement or instrument that would reduce the trust's entitlement to ordinary shares, voting rights, distributable profits or assets on a winding up without the trustee's consent.

There is one modification to this to cover a situation where the trustee borrows money from a third party. For example, the trustee of an employee ownership trust might borrow from a bank to purchase shares and the bank might require security for its loan in the form of a charge (mortgage)  over the trust's shares, which enables the bank to acquire full ownership of the shares and therefore control of the company if the trustees breach the terms of the loan. If the lender is a genuine third party this is permitted but it would not be if the "lender" was a person who sold their shares to the trust on terms that payment for them was deferred.

Where a seller takes a charge over the shares it has sold, this would need to be limited in its scope so that the charge could not be enforced over all the trust's shares, only over such number as, if enforced, would still leave the trust with a controlling interest.

## (d) The trading requirement

The *trading requirement* for the purposes of the CGT relief is that C must either be a trading company or the *principal company* of a trading group.

The trading requirement for income tax purposes is similar but not identical. C must either be a trading company or *the member of a trading group.*

### (i) Why the difference?

A seller of shares to an employee ownership trust wishing to claim the CGT relief must sell shares in the top company of the group, not a subsidiary, whereas the income tax relief could be made available to employees of a subsidiary.

### (ii) Trading company

This is rather baldly defined as a company that carries on trading activities and does not to a substantial extent carry out non-trading activities.

The trade must be conducted on a commercial basis with a view to profits.

Merely preparing to carry on a trade or to acquire a trade or a trading company is not enough: the company must actually be trading.

The definitions of "principal company of a trading group" and "member of a trading group" are those in TCGA 1992, section 170.

## 6.2 The CGT relief

The CGT relief is available to a person (P) disposing of shares in a company (C) to an employee ownership trust on or after 6 April 2014.

A company may not claim the relief, although HM Revenue and Customs have granted a concession which extends the relief to a corporate trustee.

A transitional relief is available for disposals which took place between 6 April and 26 June 2014, which was the date on which certain amendments to the Finance Bill 2014 were published.

### (a) How does the relief work?

A disposal to an employee ownership trust is treated as being made on a no gain/no loss basis. This means that:

The transferor will not be charged to CGT on the disposal; and

The trustee will be deemed to acquire the shares for the transferor's base cost.

### (b) The relief requirements

There are five requirements for claiming CGT relief:
- trading
- all-employee benefit
- controlling interest
- limited participation
- no related disposal.

### (i) Trading requirement

The company (C) must meet the trading requirement when the disposal occurs, and must continue to do so until the end of the tax year. For more information, see *Trading requirement* in 6.1(d).

### (ii) All-employee benefit requirement

The trust must meet the all-employee benefit requirement when the disposal occurs and must continue to do so until the end of the tax year. For more information, see *All-employee benefit requirement* in 6.1(a)

### (iii) Controlling interest requirement

The trust:

**Must not meet the controlling interest requirement** immediately before the beginning of the tax year in which the disposal is made; but

**Must meet the controlling interest requirement** at some point during or at the end of the tax year in which the disposal occurs.

For more information, see *Controlling interest requirement* in 6.1(c).

Once the controlling interest requirement has been met, it must continue to do so until the end of the tax year.

The tax relief works in this way so that the trustee may acquire, during a tax year, shares from different shareholders at different stages and all those selling shareholders may claim the CGT relief.

### (iv) Limited participation requirement

Under the limited participation requirement, two conditions must be satisfied.

Their purpose is to ensure that the CGT relief may only be claimed in respect of shares in a company which has a minimum number of genuine employees who are not also material shareholders or their relatives. The policy objective of the relief is to encourage the growth of employee ownership by increasing the number of employees who have an ownership stake in their company.

| Condition A | Condition B |
|---|---|
| At no time in the 12 months ending immediately after the disposal to the trust were both the following true: | At no time in the period beginning with the disposal and ending at the end of tax year in which the disposal took place did the participator fraction exceed 2/5 |
| P (the person claiming the relief) is a 5% participator in C (the company) | However, the relief may still be available even if the participator fraction is more than 2/5, if this is for a period of no more than six months and it is because of events outside the reasonable control of the trustees |
| The participator fraction is more than 2/5. | |

What is the Participator fraction?

The participator fraction means **NP/NE**, where:

**NP** is the sum of:

- the number of people who are both 5% participators in C and employees or directors or company secretary (officeholders) of C; and
- the number of people who are employees or directors of C or a member of C's group, and connected[13] with another employee or officeholder who is a 5% participator.

**NE** means the total number of the group's employees.

**Participator** has the meaning given by CTA 2010, section 454. However, if C is not a close company it includes anyone who would be a participator if it were a close company.

**5% participator** means a participator who is entitled to or has rights to acquire 5% or more of any class of C's share capital or would be entitled to 5% of more of the assets on a winding up of C.

### (v) No related disposal requirement
Neither P (the person claiming the relief) nor any person connected with P shall have claimed the same CGT relief in any earlier year in relation to any disposal of shares in the same company or any member of the same group.

### (c) How to claim the relief
A person who has sold shares to an employee ownership trust and wishes to claim CGT relief should do so in the capital gains pages of their self-assessment tax return and then the relief claimed by inserting the three-letter code for the relief. Our understanding is that this should be *OTH* for "other claims", as there is no specific code for relief for disposal to an employee ownership trust. The white space of the same form should then be used to provide full details of the relief claimed (see *HMRC: Capital gains tax summary notes, 6 April 2017*).

---

[13] *Connected* means an Individual's spouse, civil partner, relative (brother, sister, ancestor, lineal descendant) or spouse or civil partner of a relative of an individual or of an individual's spouse or civil partner.

**Working out the participator fraction in your company**

*Health warning; this is a simplified approach*:

First, add up :

- *The number of people who are both 5% shareholders and employees/office holders; and*
- *The number of **other** people who are both employees/office holders (including all companies in the same group) and connected\* with the persons above.*

The total of these is **NP**.

Second, add up *total number of group employees.* This gives you **NE**.

*The ratio between NP and NE must not be more than 2/5.*

### (d) The relief is clawed back if a disqualifying event occurs up to the end of the following tax year

Every potential seller to an employee ownership trust should be aware, if they are planning to claim CGT relief, that they will not be able to do so if a *disqualifying event* occurs between the date of sale and the end of the following tax year.

It is recommended that a shareholder selling to an employee ownership trust considers including in their contract with the trust an agreement with both the trustees and the company that, so far as possible, no action will be taken that would result in a disqualifying event.

### (e) The trust is liable for CGT if a disqualifying event occurs after the end of the following tax year

If a disqualifying event occurs following the end of the tax year after the one in which the CGT relief is claimed the trustees will be deemed to have disposed of, and then reacquired, all the shares in respect of which the relief was claimed. This means that there is a CGT charge on the market value of the shares at that time less the vendor's original base cost.

There are situations where a tax liability could arise on the trustees as a result of them losing control of the company, but where they do not have the funds to pay it, for example if the company has issued new shares.

## What is a disqualifying event?

Any of the following will be a disqualifying event:

- *C ceases to meet the trading requirement*
- *the EOT ceases to meet the all-employee benefit requirement*
- *the EOT ceases to meet the controlling interest requirement*
- *the participator fraction exceeds 2/5*
- *the trustees act in a way which infringes the all-employee benefit requirement.*

## (i) *How concerned should the trustees of an employee ownership trust be about this potential CGT liability?*

It is suggested that in practice this will either be within the trustees' control or, if a disqualifying event takes place for reasons beyond their control, a CGT liability is generally unlikely to result.

Considering each of the disqualifying events in turn:

*C ceases to meet the trading requirement.* It should be within the control of the trustees as majority shareholders to ensure that the company's directors do not change the business to such an extent that it is no longer trading.

If the company ceases trading due to insolvency, it is likely that it will then have little or no value. The likely effect is that the trust's shares will themselves have little or no value, which will mean there will not be any CGT liability. CGT is charged on the difference between the base cost of the original shareholders (i.e. what their shares were worth when they originally acquired them) and their market value when the company ceased trading.

*The EOT ceases to meet the all-employee benefit requirement.* This will only happen if the terms of the trust deed are changed. A properly drafted employee ownership trust deed should require the trustees' agreement to any change, giving them the power to ensure that it does not happen. Further, it is at least good practice for a trust deed to prohibit a change which would mean the all-employee benefit requirement ceased to be met.

*The EOT ceases to meet the controlling interest requirement.* This could happen in two main ways. First, the trustees could agree to sell a controlling interest in the company to a third party. This would be their decision and they would do so knowing that a CGT liability may arise as a result. Second, the company could issue new shares to other persons, diluting the trust's holding so that it no longer had control. This can be prevented by the trustees requiring, as controlling shareholders, that this is a "reserved matter" which would require their consent.

*The participator fraction exceeds 2/5.* There are two ways in which this could happen. First, the company could issue new shares to individuals, who each become a 5% participator, resulting in the numerator in the participator fraction exceeding 2. The trustees can prevent this happening by, as explained above, ensuring their consent must be sought before any new issue of shares. Second, the number of employees could fall to such an extent that the denominator falls below 5. This may not be within the control of the trustees. However if the number of employees fell to this extent it is generally likely that the size of the company's business activities will have become so small that there is no longer any material value in the company, and so no liability to CGT.

*The trustees act in a way which infringes the all-employee benefit requirement.* This will be within the control of the trustees. If at any stage they are not clear how they should operate the trust within the all employee benefit requirement, they should take professional advice.

### (ii) Can a CGT liability be legally avoided by locating an employee ownership trust offshore?

The risk of a CGT liability on the trust can be avoided by locating the trust offshore so that it is not UK resident. However, careful consideration should be given to whether it is appropriate to have offshore trustees of an employee ownership trust.

A key role of an employee ownership trust will generally be to foster employee engagement in the company and its business, which arguably can much more effectively be performed where the trustees themselves are engaged and have a strong commitment to successful employee ownership. This may be more likely where trustees are drawn from employees and one or more independents, sometimes joined by a former shareholder or member of the senior leadership team, all of whom can attend trustee meetings on the company's premises and be in regular direct contact with employees and the company's senior leaders.

Where a trust has offshore trustees, these will need to be professional trustees who will likely be acting as trustees for a significant number of other trusts. Trustee meetings will need to be held where the trustees are resident, for example the Channel Islands or Isle of Man, with no regular on the ground contact between trustees and people in the company. Significant professional trustee costs are likely to be involved.

For these reasons, it is suggested that notwithstanding the potential CGT advantage of choosing to locate an employee ownership trust outside the UK, it will generally be better not to do so.

### (f) Transfers between trusts
The CGT relief is also available if an employee ownership trust becomes absolutely entitled to shares held in another trust.

The effect is that there is a deemed disposal of those shares (*TCGA 1992, section 71*). This could for example happen if an owner of a company put shares into a family trust, with the remainder to an employee ownership trust.

If CGT relief is to be claimed in respect of such a transfer, the employee ownership trust and the company must meet the first four of the relief requirements:
- trading
- all-employee benefit
- controlling interest
- limited participation.

The no related disposal requirement does not apply.

As with the CGT relief on disposals by individuals to an employee ownership trust, the relief will be clawed back from the trustees who transferred shares to the employee ownership trust if there is a disqualifying event up to the end of the following tax year.

## 6.3 Income tax free bonus payments

Employees of a company (or of a subsidiary of a holding company) owned by an employee ownership trust can be paid income tax free bonus payments of up to £3,600 per tax year.

These must be paid by the employee company, not the employee ownership trust.

National Insurance contributions still have to be paid.

### (a) Requirements for the relief

These are the requirements for the income tax relief to be available:

- the £3,600 limit
- payment must not be regular wages or salary
- the participation requirement
- the equality requirement
- the trading requirement
- the indirect employee-ownership requirement
- the officeholder requirement
- employer company must not be a service company
- the bonus must not be an excluded payment
- the bonus must not be paid to a former employee more than 12 months after cessation of employment.

Each of these is considered below.

### (i) The £3,600 limit

An income tax free bonus payment to an employee must not exceed £3,600 per tax year.

### (ii) The payment must not be regular wages or salary

The payment must not be regular wages or salary. This is not defined but the clear objective is to ensure that income tax relief applies only to genuine bonuses. So-called "salary sacrifice" arrangements under which employees trade regular salary for a guaranteed bonus may not be paid income tax free.

### (iii) The participation requirement

The payment must be made under a *scheme* that meets the participation requirement. The legislation does not say what is required for there to be a "scheme". It is recommended to set out in writing how each employee's entitlement to the bonus is determined and any eligibility requirements (for example, length of service – see below).

To satisfy the participation requirement, all employees of the company (or all group employees) must be eligible to participate in any award under the scheme.

Those who are *excluded participators* and so not beneficiaries of the employee ownership trust  (see 6.1(a)(i)) are nonetheless eligible to receive income tax free bonuses.

There are two exceptions:

The scheme can exclude newly recruited employees, by allowing a company to limit participation to employees who have completed a minimum period of continuous service. This may be set at up to 12 months. The same period does not have to be used for each payment. For example, in one year the qualifying period could be 12 months and the next year it could be changed to six. It is not recommended, however, to make frequent changes to the qualifying period; and

Employees can be excluded on disciplinary grounds. More specifically:

Where an employee is subject to disciplinary proceedings, their entitlement can be suspended, any payment to be conditional on there being no finding of gross misconduct;

Where, between the date when the amount of the payment is determined and when it is paid, disciplinary proceedings take place, if there is a finding of gross misconduct or summary dismissal, the employee will be deemed never to have been eligible to receive the payment if the employee is found to have committed gross misconduct in the 12 months before the award was determined, they can be denied the right to receive payment.

### (iv)  Equality requirement
The payment must be made under a scheme that meets the equality requirement. See 6.1(b).

## (v) Trading requirement

The employer company must have been a trading company or a member of a trading group throughout a qualifying period.

(see *Trading requirement*, above and *qualifying period* (below).

## (vi) Indirect employee-ownership requirement

This test requires the employer company (or its holding company) to be majority owned by a trust which is for the benefit of all employees on the same terms.

More precisely, the trust must:
- meet the all-employee benefit requirement (see 6.1(a)); and
- meet the controlling interest requirement (see 6.1(c)) throughout a qualifying period.

*"Qualifying period"* means the period of twelve months ending with the date when the payment is made. (However, if the controlling interest requirement or the all-employee benefit requirement is first met during the 12 month period, it is not necessary for that requirement to have been met for a full twelve months).

## (vii) Officeholder requirement

This has some similarities to the participator fraction (see 6.2(b)(iv)) but its purpose is to ensure that the company has a minimum number of genuine employees compared with directors and other officers rather than shareholders.

The calculation must be done in relation to the company whose employees are intended to receive the income tax bonus. So where there is a group of companies, each with its own employees, the calculation must be done for each company.

The officeholder requirement stipulates that the ratio of office holders and directors to total employees must not exceed 2/5:
- at the time the bonus is paid; and
- For a requisite number of days in the qualifying period.

As with the indirect employee ownership requirement, the qualifying period is normally the 12-month period ending with the payment of the bonus. However, if either the controlling interest requirement or the all-employee benefit requirement is first met during that 12-month period, the qualifying period does not include the time before that requirement was met.

Where the qualifying period is twelve months, the requisite number of days is 12 months less 90 days. Where the qualifying period is less than twelve months, it is reduced proportionately.

**Working out the officeholder requirement in your company**

*As with the participator fraction, this is a simplified approach*:

First, add up:

*Number of people who are directors/office holders of the Company; and/or*

*Number of employees connected\* with any of them*

The total of these is **ND**

Second, Add up number of employee or office holders of the Company. This gives you **NE**

*The ratio between ND and NE must not be more than 2/5.*

*\*(Connected means Individual's spouse, civil partner, relative (brother, sister, ancestor, lineal descendant) or spouse or civil partner of a relative of individual or of individual's spouse or civil partner.*

*(viii)   The employer company must not be a service company*

The employer company must not be a *service company*, that is, a company a substantial part of whose business is providing the services of people employed by it mainly to persons who control it (or used to control it), but who are not members of the same group as the employer company.

A *managed service company* (*ITEPA 2003, section 61B*) is treated as a service company.

*(ix)  The bonus must not be an excluded payment*

The payment must not be funded through salary, bonus or benefit sacrifice, for example through a flexible benefits plan.

*(x)   Bonus must not be paid to former employee more than 12 months after cessation of employment*

It is permitted (but not required) to pay a bonus to a former employee, or to the estate of a deceased employee, so long as not more than 12 months have passed after the employment ceased or the employee died.

## 6.4   Inheritance tax reliefs

Inheritance tax legislation was amended at the same time as the CGT and income tax reliefs relating to employee ownership trusts were introduced. The effects are considered below.

### (a)  Transfer by close company to employee ownership trust

A transfer of property by a close company[14] to an employee ownership trust is not treated as a *transfer of value* for inheritance tax purposes, provided the following conditions are met:

- *the company must be a trading company (or the principal company of a trading group);*
- *the trust must meet the all-employee benefit requirement; and*
- *the trust does not meet the controlling interest requirement at the beginning of the tax year in which the transfer occurs, but does meet it by the end of the tax year.*

*(Inheritance Tax Act 1984, section 13A)*

### (b)  Transfer of shares by individual to employee ownership trust

A transfer of shares in a company by an individual to an employee ownership trust is exempt from inheritance tax where:

- *the company meets the trading requirement;*
- *the employee ownership trust meets the all-employee benefit requirement; and*
- *the employee ownership trust does not meet the controlling interest requirement immediately before the tax year in which the share transfer is made but does meet it at the end of that tax year.*

*(IHTA 1984, section 28A)*

### (c)  Relief from exit charge for relevant property trusts

The relief under *IHTA 1984, section 86* from the exit charge on shares or securities held in a *relevant property trust* (this means a trust holding *relevant property*, which means property that is not, broadly, beneficially owned by any particular person) where those shares or

---

[14] A close company is a company controlled by (broadly) five or fewer shareholders.

securities cease to be relevant property, is extended so that it also applies to employee ownership trusts, subject to the following conditions:

- *the company meets the **trading requirement**;*
- *the employee ownership trust meets the **all-employee benefit requirement**; and*
- *the employee ownership trust does not meet the **controlling interest requirement** immediately before the tax year in which the shares or securities cease to be relevant property but does meet it at the end of that tax year.*

*(IHTA 1984, section 75A).*

An employee ownership trust is regarded as complying with IHTA 1984, section 86. This section sets out the requirements for an employee trust to be exempt from a ten-yearly charge to inheritance tax and an exit charge on distributions from a trust.

There will be no inheritance tax exit charge under IHTA 1984, section 72 if the trust property ceases to be held in an EOT where this is due to the trust no longer meeting the controlling interest requirement or the all-employee benefit requirement *(IHTA 1984, section 72(3A)).*

A commentary from HMRC on inheritance tax and employee ownership trusts is available. Please see *HMRC: Inheritance Tax Manual: IHTM42995-42997.*

**To recap:**
- For either CGT exemption or income tax relief to be available:
  - *the EOT's assets must be held for the benefit of all employees (up to 12 months' qualifying period allowed)*
  - *this must be on a "same terms" basis*
  - *the EOT must control the company*
  - *the company must be trading.*
- For the CGT relief to be available, the ratio between (simplified version) (i) people who are both 5%+ shareholders and directors/company secretary/employees and (ii) employees must not be more than 2/5 (this is to prevent the relief being

claimed in companies where there are few non-shareholder employees).

- The CGT relief is clawed back if there is a *disqualifying event.*
- For the income tax relief to be available:
  - *the company (or its holding company) must be controlled by an EOT*
  - *bonuses must be paid to all (qualifying) employees on a same terms basis*
  - *ratio between (again, simplified version) people who are (i) directors/company secretary and (ii) employees/directors/company secretary must not be more than 2/5 (to prevent the relief being claimed in companies where there are few employees who are not also officers of the company (i.e. directors or company secretary).*
- There are additional requirements for the income tax relief.
- Inheritance reliefs are also available.

# 7 Ownership succession by transfer to an employee ownership trust

This chapter sets out the key practical questions and steps a company's shareholder(s) will need to consider and work through if they wish to arrange ownership succession in their company by transfer to an employee ownership trust.

If an *employee benefit trust* is chosen instead, many of the same steps will apply, but it will not be necessary to consider the employee ownership trust tax conditions.

We start with a flowchart setting out the main steps in planning (see page opposite).

## 7.1 Have the qualification requirements for an employee ownership trust been met?

These are considered in Chapter 6.

## 7.2 Key financial questions

The four questions below should preferably be considered together as they are interconnected. Once they have been addressed, this will enable the terms of the purchase to be recorded in a share purchase agreement (see 7.9).

### (a) What is the value of the shares to be bought?

An independent valuation of the company will be required, because:

- the trustees will wish to be confident that they are not paying a price for the shares they are buying which is more than their market value (if they do pay more than market value, they will be in breach of trust), or
- if the sale price is greater than market value, the selling shareholders will be liable for income tax on the surplus.

Where the trust is to purchase less than a 100% holding, the value of the shares it is to buy may not necessarily directly correlate with the percentage of shares it is buying. For example, if it is to purchase 51% of a company worth £1 million, the value of that 51% holding may not be £510,000 but may instead be discounted to an amount

## Planning ownership succession by share transfer to an employee trust

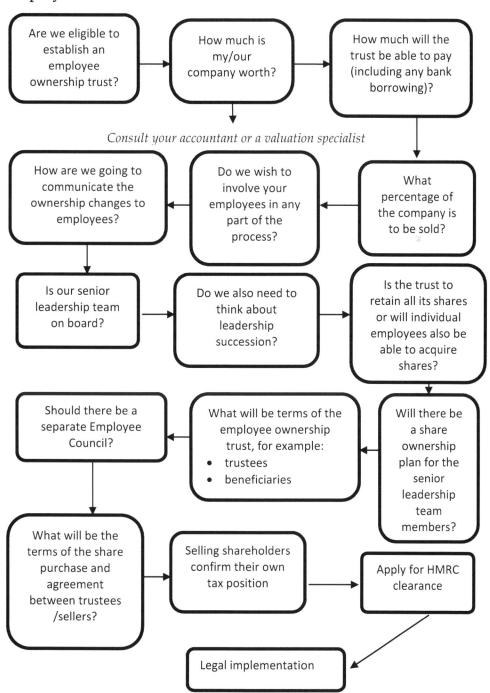

Are we eligible to establish an employee ownership trust? → How much is my/our company worth? → How much will the trust be able to pay (including any bank borrowing)?

*Consult your accountant or a valuation specialist*

How are we going to communicate the ownership changes to employees? ← Do we wish to involve your employees in any part of the process? ← What percentage of the company is to be sold?

Is our senior leadership team on board? → Do we also need to think about leadership succession? → Is the trust to retain all its shares or will individual employees also be able to acquire shares?

Should there be a separate Employee Council? ← What will be terms of the employee ownership trust, for example:
- trustees
- beneficiaries
← Will there be a share ownership plan for the senior leadership team members?

What will be the terms of the share purchase and agreement between trustees /sellers? → Selling shareholders confirm their own tax position → Apply for HMRC clearance

Legal implementation

between, say, £400,000 and £450,000. This is because a 51% holding does not give its holder full control and it may be more difficult to sell the shares compared with if it had a 100% holding.

Shareholders contemplating selling less than 100% should also be aware that a discount may apply in the same way if they sell their retained shares in the future and they will not be able to claim capital gains relief on any such future sale (unless it takes place within the same tax year as the first sale).

### (b) How much will the trust be able to pay?

The trust will be relying on receiving payments from the company to fund its purchase price. Generally, it is likely that these will be paid out of the company's future profits, although in some cases the company may have surplus cash which can be used to fund a down payment.

Each payment by the company must always be funded out of distributable profits.

If the trust, or the company, is to borrow funds from a bank or other third party to contribute towards the purchase price (see below), the interest and capital repayments on that borrowing will be funded by the company.

It is therefore recommended to model the company's anticipated future cashflow and profit so that a plan and timetable can be created for funding payments of purchase price and/or repayments of borrowing and interest.

### (c) Will any external borrowing be required to fund the purchase price?

An increasing number of banks and other borrowers are familiar with employee ownership and willing to lend to help fund the purchase price. A business owner planning a sale to an employee ownership trust may, if they wish to maximise the amount of the purchase price to be paid on completion, consider the feasibility of external funding.

Potential lenders are likely to apply normal criteria in assessing whether to offer a loan, including the strength of the senior leadership, cash flow cover, and the availability of security.

If security is sought over the shares the trust is to purchase, care is needed. If a lender could potentially take control of the company in the event of loan default, the controlling interest requirement would not be met (see Chapter 6) and neither the EOT CGT or income tax reliefs would be available.

**(d) What percentage of the company's shares are to be sold?**
An employee ownership trust must acquire more than 50% of the shares in the company if the CGT and income tax reliefs are to be available.

This gives a clear choice to the retiring owner(s). Shall they sell 50.1%, 100% or a percentage in between?

In making a decision, these are some factors that could be taken into account:
- *What percentage can the trust afford to buy?*
- *Do the current owners wish to hold back some shares for acquisition by leadership team members?*
- *Do the current owners wish to retain an investment in the company?*
- *Do the current owners wish to claim CGT relief on all their shares? (If they do, they will need to give up a controlling interest and sell all their remaining shares in a single tax year)*
- *Do the current owners wish to avoid a minority discount affecting the value of any shares they sell? (If so, they should sell all their shares in a single transaction).*

## 7.3   How consultative will the process be?
It will be important for any retiring owner to gain support for a change to employee ownership from the company's senior leadership team. Once a clear plan is in place, at the very least it should be presented to the senior leaders with full and clear opportunity for them to ask questions. This may require a significant commitment of time and energy if it is to be done well.

There is an argument in favour of going beyond this and consulting with senior leadership team members on key aspects of the plan.

After all, they will have the task of making it work. Not all retiring owners wish to do this, though, particularly where they have firm and confident views as to how the ownership change should be structured.

A company wishing to be as consultative as possible might consider going one stage further and involve representatives of employees as a whole in certain parts of the ownership design. For example, where this is done it might include consultation on how employee views on business improvement can most effectively be communicated to the leadership team and how any resulting discussion should be organised.

All of this, and other vital people issues are considered further in Chapter 9.

## 7.4  How are the employees to be engaged in being owners?

It will be critical to the successful introduction and operation of employee ownership in any company that the employees understand what it means and how it works.

Knowledge levels and familiarity with employee ownership will increase over time and it is unrealistic to expect every employee to understand everything from day one. It will be a gradual process, involving frequent and clear communication and an all round commitment to engaging employees as owners.

After a period, both senior leaders, trustees and employees should begin to develop an employee ownership "muscle memory", so that it becomes more instinctive.

## 7.5  Is the trust to retain all its shares or should there be a hybrid form of employee ownership in which all employees are also able to acquire shares personally?

This is discussed in Chapter 2.

## 7.6  Are senior leadership team members supportive?

It will be essential for directors/senior leadership team members to support the transition.

## 7.7    Leadership succession

Where an existing owner plays a critical role in the company's leadership and intends stepping back (or stepping down) it will be important to have a plan for leadership succession.

## 7.8    Are senior leadership team members to have their own share ownership plan?

This is discussed in Chapter 2.

If it is felt important that continuing directors (and possibly other senior managers) have their own personal ownership stake, this can done.

Where shares are to offered to certain employees only, the *all-employee benefit* requirement (see Chapter 6) means that they cannot be supplied by an employee ownership trust.

The alternatives are:
- *the company issues new shares; or*
- *the retiring owners retain some of their shares which they transfer directly to selected employees (or grant options over them).*

## 7.9    The employee ownership trust

There follow some key questions on how the trust will be structured:

### (a)  Who will be its trustees?

This is considered in Chapter 3.

### (b)  Who will be its beneficiaries?

### (i)  *When it matters who the trust's beneficiaries are*

In practice, this question is likely only to have practical relevance if:
- *the trust is ever to transfer property (generally cash or shares) to beneficiaries; or*
- *the trust ever comes to an end.*

Considering each in turn:

**Trust transferring property:** As bonuses or profit shares will generally be paid directly to employees by the company rather than through the trust, it is unlikely that during the life of an employee ownership trust it will be paying cash to beneficiaries.

Where there is hybrid employee ownership, involving both trust and individual share ownership, this will normally involve the trust transferring shares to employees. So in practice the question of who is a beneficiary will have importance in these circumstances.

**The trust comes to an end:** If the trust is ever terminated (most likely if the trust sells the company) and the trust deed requires net sale proceeds (after taxation and expenses) to be distributed to beneficiaries, it is clearly going to be important to identify who is a beneficiary.

### (ii) Who can be a beneficiary

Whilst the employee ownership trust legislation requires that all the company's employees be beneficiaries, this is subject to the following:

- *it is possible to require an employee to have worked for the company for a minimum continuous period, which can be up to twelve months;*
- *dependants of a deceased employee can be beneficiaries (but do not have to be);*
- *office holders who are not employees (in practice, this is most likely to mean non-executive directors and freelance company secretaries) can be beneficiaries (but do not have to be);*
- *if the company has ceased to be a trading company or the trust no longer holds any shares in the company, any individual who has been an eligible employee for the preceding two years continues to be a beneficiary; and*
- *excluded participators may not be beneficiaries (see Chapter 6).*

### (c) How should trustee decisions be made?

Should trustee decisions be made by majority vote or should unanimity be required? Where a trust has individual trustees rather than a corporate trustee (see Chapter 4), the default requirement will be unanimity unless the trust deed specifies otherwise.

It is possible to stipulate different levels of trustee approval depending on the matter they are considering. For example, the trust deed could say that generally trustee decisions can be made by majority vote but certain key decisions (for example, to sell the company) would require unanimity.

### (d) Should there be a separate Employee Council?

In any successful employee-owned company, strong and effective communication between the company's directors, the trustees and the beneficiaries will be critical.

For a company which has a large number of employees, or operates from several locations, it may be useful to set up an *Employee Council*. This would typically comprise a group of employees, elected by the employees as a whole, whose role would be to listen to any questions and concerns that employees have as employee owners, and then raise them with the trustees. Once the trustees have discussed any particular issue raised by the Employee Council, they would feed back their response to the Council, the members of which would then pass that back to employees as a whole.

It would not be the role of an Employee Council (or trustees) to consider individual employee grievances or the minutiae of running the business. Its central role is more likely to relate to questions relating to ownership, for example:

- *identifying where employees do not feel engaged in the business and how to address this;*
- *listening to employees' questions and suggestions about improvements as to how the company operates;*
- *consulting with the trustees to help the trustees make decision on major questions; and*
- *acting as the eyes and ears of the trustees, ensuring that the trustees are connected with how employees see the business and their role in it.*

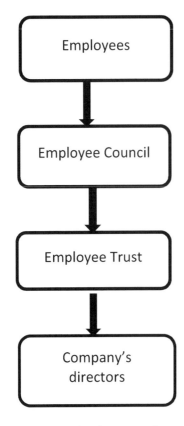

| | |
|---|---|
| **Employees** | |
| ↓ | |
| **Employee Council** | *Listens to questions, ideas and concerns of employees. Decides which ones should be raised with trustees. Feeds back to employees* |
| ↓ | |
| **Employee Trust** | *Discuss any matters raised by Employee Council. Responds or raises them with company's directors (and then responds)* |
| ↓ | |
| **Company's directors** | *Listens to points raised by trustees and responds. Take action where appropriate.* |

## (e) Should the trust's permission be required for particular actions?

Whilst the company will be run on a day to day basis by its directors, there will from time to time be a need to make a major decision which is important enough to justify trustee involvement.

When the trust is established, it is common to create a list of steps which would require trust approval, for example the company acquiring another business or appointing or removing any director.

## (f) Insurance

It is recommended that trustees (or directors of a corporate trustee) have the benefit of a directors' and officers' insurance policy. Premiums do not tend to be high and such a policy will give important comfort to trustees – many of whom will initially be unfamiliar with the role – that they have protection from personal liability that this kind of policy brings.

## (g) What should happen if the trust ever comes to an end?

The trust deed should specify what will happen to the assets of the trust if it is terminated.

Were this to happen, it is most likely that it would be following a sale by the trust of all of its shares in the company. After paying the expenses of the sale and any CGT, the following could apply to the net sale proceeds:

- *distributed to employees on the same terms or*
- *given to charity or*
- *a combination of the above.*

## 7.10  HM Revenue and Customs clearance

UK tax legislation contains anti-avoidance provisions relating to "disguised dividend". Just as a company's shareholders who receive a dividend must pay income tax on it, if shareholders receive a payment which has the same effect as a dividend even though it does not immediately look like one, it will often still be income taxable.

For example, if a company funds a trust (out of its profits), and the trust then pays that money on to a shareholder, at first sight that would be a "disguised dividend" and would result in an income tax liability for that shareholder.

Shareholders selling to an employee trust will generally be looking for their tax treatment to be CGT rather than income tax, and if the purchaser is an employee ownership trust they will be seeking an exemption from CGT.

The anti-avoidance provisions do not apply if a main purpose of the transaction is not the obtaining of an income tax advantage. So where shareholders are giving up control of their company as part of an ownership succession plan, HM Revenue and Customs will often accept that there should be no income tax charge. This will depend on the circumstances and it will generally be necessary to show that there is a change of control of the company. An advance clearance procedure is available.

Where the result of a sale is that current shareholders' reduce their holding to no more than 25% of the company,[15] this is regarded as a "fundamental change of ownership" and the anti-avoidance provisions are automatically disapplied. In principle, this should mean that advance clearance is not required, although many practitioners continue to apply for advance clearance for certainty.

## 7.11 Terms of the share purchase

The terms of the trust's share purchase will need to be recorded in a written agreement.

### (a) Price and payment terms

The agreement will need to specify the total purchase price and how this is to be paid. Generally, this is likely to be in instalments, with the company funding the trust from future profits, which the trust then uses to pay instalments of the purchase price.

The payment terms should be flexible enough to accommodate potential fluctuations in the company's future profitability and cash flows, and it is likely that the trustees' will want their liability to pay a given instalment always to be conditional on them having received the funds with which to do so.

Shareholders selling to the trust can stipulate that interest should be paid on the unpaid purchase price, or alternatively interest should be paid on any purchase price instalments which fall behind schedule.

If selling shareholders are concerned that the trust may sell the company after a short period and make a capital gain, the purchase agreement could include an additional provision giving the selling shareholders the right to a percentage of the trust's net gain if it sells on within a defined period.

### (b) Reserved matters

Although shareholders selling a majority shareholding to an employee trust must accept that they are giving up control (and if the trust is an employee ownership trust, this is a condition of the

---

[15] This is only a summary of the requirements, which are more detailed and can be found in Income Tax Act 2007, section 686.

associated tax reliefs), they can specify that their permission will be required if the company is to take certain defined steps, which may give some assurance that the company will be properly and profitably run, and that it will be able to fund the trust to pay purchase price instalments.

This is a similar concept to the trust's rights under 7.9(e), although the trust's rights will be permanent whereas the sellers' rights should cease once they have been paid in full.

If this approach is taken it is likely that there will be several items requiring the sellers' approval, for example the company incurring capital expenditure in a single year over a specified amount and the trust selling any of its shares. It is important not to include anything on this sellers' approval list that may suggest the sellers still have active control of the company, for example the right to appoint or remove directors.

## (c) Warranties

It is common for selling shareholders give warranties in the purchase agreement. These take the form of a series of statements about the company which are designed to reassure the trustees, as purchasers, that there are no skeletons in the cupboard.

For example, warranties might include statements that the company's accounts (upon which any valuation will have been based) are accurate, that all taxes have been paid and that the company is not involved in any litigation.

The warranties become terms of the contract so that if any of them are not correct, that will be a breach of contract by the selling shareholders.

As the trustees will generally include individuals who do not have an inside knowledge of the company, it will usually be essential that they have the benefit of warranties.

Where the trust is being given the shares, warranties may not be relevant and, if the purchase price is less than market value, the selling shareholders' financial liability under warranties will often be reduced to reflect that.

### (d) Protection against forfeiture of CGT relief

Selling shareholders may also consider including in the agreement undertakings from both the trust and the company that they will not take steps that would result in a *disqualifying event* (see Chapter 6) up to the end of the following tax year. If a disqualifying event were to occur within that period, selling shareholders would forfeit their exemption from capital gains.

### (e) Non-compete covenants

Depending on the circumstances, the trustees may wish the share purchase agreement to contain a promise by the selling shareholders that they will not set up or work in a competing business, nor poach employees, customers or suppliers, for a defined period after the sale. In practice, where selling shareholders are being paid in instalments it is unlikely that it would be in their interests to do so, but there may be circumstances where this is relevant.

## 7.12 Selling shareholders' tax position

Each selling shareholder should take their own personal advice on their tax treatment, in the context of their wider estate planning.

Where the purchase price is to be paid in instalments (effectively, an IOU from the trust as purchaser to each selling shareholder) and an individual who has sold their shares dies before having been paid in full, the value of any unpaid instalments will be treated as part of their estate for inheritance tax purposes. This is fundamentally different from what the position would have been if they had retained their shares, as the shares would generally then be exempt from inheritance tax under business property relief.

It is important that each selling shareholder is aware of this and that in the event of their untimely death, planning has been done to ensure that the estate will have funds available to pay any inheritance tax liability.

## 7.13 Independent advice for trustees?

Becoming a trustee is a significant responsibility. Training for trustees is recommended, but a company moving to employee ownership should also consider providing the trustees with the opportunity to obtain their own advice on the terms of the trust deed, the intended share purchase and other aspects of the transition to employee ownership, and should set aside a budget to cover the costs.

## 7.14  Stamp duty

In order to formally transfer their shares to the purchasing trust, each selling shareholder will need to sign a short stock transfer form. For the transfer to have legal effect, stamp duty must be paid on the total purchase price (whether or not it is paid in full on the transfer date) within 28 days. This is at the rate of 0.5% of the purchase price in each transfer form, rounded up to the nearest £5 of duty.

For example, if the purchase price receivable by a selling shareholder is £351,500, the duty will be £1,760.

## 7.15  The process

The key steps in arranging a sale to an employee ownership trust:

## DESIGN
Valuation
Purchase price
Consider borrowing
How many shares to be sold?
Consult with employees?
Communication and
engagement
Terms of the employee trust
Are all shares to remain in
trust or will there be
individual share ownership?
Employee Council?
Terms of the share purchase
Selling shareholders' tax
position
Consider any management
succession issues

## LEGAL IMPLEMENTATION
HMRC clearance
Trust deed
Share purchase agreement
New articles of association
Form trustee company
Shareholders' agreement?
Ancillary documents
Final employee
communications
Appoint trustees

## COMPLETION
Set up trust – sign trust deed
Sign purchase agreement
Sign other documents
Board and trustee meetings
to approve transaction

## POST-COMPLETION
Pay stamp duty
Companies House filings etc
Tell your clients
Tell your employees
Focus on employee
engagement
Financial reporting to
employees
Regular trustee meetings
Regular directors' meetings

# 8 Anatomy of an employee ownership trust deed

This chapter considers some of the most common provisions found in a trust deed creating an employee ownership trust.

No two trust deeds will be alike and different lawyers will have their own drafting styles. Whilst all employee ownership trust deeds may to a large extent contain similar provisions, the order in which they are set out will not always be the same and there will always be provisions which are unique to a particular trust.

For these reasons this chapter considers the main provisions which may be found in a trust deed but does not attribute to them particular trust deed clause numbers.

## 8.1 Principal clauses

| Provision | What it means |
|---|---|
| *Interpretation* | This sets out a number of words of phrases used later in the trust deed and says what they mean. Often they will be capitalised, for example **Beneficiary**, and/or may be put in parentheses: **"Beneficiary"**. When reading a trust deed for the first time, it is not recommended to start with this part; it is likely to make more sense to refer back to it when reading the rest of the trust deed. |
| *Beneficiaries* | This sets out who are the beneficiaries of the trust. It will ensure compliance with the employee ownership trust tax legislation, which requires that all a company's employees (or all those who have worked for a qualifying period which can be set at up to twelve months) be included as beneficiaries. |
| *Discretionary trust of capital and income* | This is core part of the trust deed. It sets out how the trust is to benefit its Beneficiaries and gives the trustees discretion as to how to do so (although as an employee ownership trust, that discretion is constrained by the fact that any benefit must be conferred on all Beneficiaries on the same terms). |
| *Perpetuity period* | This provides that the trust has a maximum life of 125 years, which is a legal requirement. |
| *Employee Council* | If the company is also to have an Employee Council, how it is to work and its purpose may be |

| | covered in a clause in the trust deed. |
|---|---|
| *Expiration of the trust period* | This clause sets out what happens at the end of the perpetuity period when the trust must come to an end (or earlier, if for example the company is sold). Any property left in the trust (generally likely to be cash after payment of tax and expenses) must either be paid to beneficiaries or paid to charity (or a combination). This clause will specify which and may go into more detail. |
| *Additions* | Under this clause, any additional property received by the trustees to be held under the trust becomes subject to the trust's terms. |
| *Powers of investment* | Under general trust law, trustees have limited powers to invest cash, so the purpose of this clause is to give them wider investment powers. |
| *Additional powers* | Trustees also have quite limited powers generally under trust law, so this clause gives them wider and extended powers to do a range of additional things. |
| *Resettlement power* | This gives the trustees power to transfer the trust's property to a separate trust. This trust must qualify as an employee ownership trust. |
| *Voting* | This clause will only be relevant if the trust holds a defined number of shares on behalf of a specific employee, i.e. it operates as a "bare trustee" where the true owner of those shares is a named employee. This is not likely to be common. Where that is the case, the trustees may only exercise voting rights over those shares according to instructions from that employee. |
| *Dealing with shares held in the trust* | Where this is included, it also covers a situation where shares are held on behalf of specific employees, as with **Voting** above, but would instead cover a situation where the trust receives an offer to sell those shares. The trustees would be required to ask any employee on whose specific behalf they held shares whether they should accept the offer on that employee's behalf. |
| *Dividend waiver* | Where the company has other shareholders as well as the trust, it may wish to pay them dividends. If the trust holds shares of the same class as those other shareholders, it will be entitled to receive |

| | dividends at the same rate per share as those other shareholders. Dividends are taxable whereas capital contributions made by the company to the trust are not, so it is common to include in the trust deed a dividend waiver, under which the trust agrees to waive its entitlement to dividend. Any funds that it would have received as a dividend will instead be paid to it as a capital contribution or, if the trust no longer needs funds to pay out previous shareholders, may instead be paid directly to employees as a bonus. |
|---|---|
| *Personal interests* | This provides for a situation where the trustees are considering a decision on a matter in which one of them has a personal interest. It will confirm whether or in what circumstances such a trustee is entitled to participate in the decision making process. |
| *Protection* | It is common for the company establishing the trust to indemnify the trustees against any personal liability incurred as a result of them making a mistake. However, this will often not extend to fraud, misconduct or negligence. |
| *Identity of trustees* | It is common, in an employee ownership trust deed, to require that trustees are drawn from certain categories of person, and to set out detailed provisions as to how and when they are to be appointed and then stand down. |
| *Trustee meetings* | The trust deed may contain rules for how trustee meetings are to be held, for example how many trustees must be present for a meeting to go ahead (quorum) and what percentage of trustees must approve any decision. |
| *Amending the trust deed* | There will normally be a clause which allows for the trust deed to be amended and which sets out how this can be done. Certain parts of an employee ownership deed, however, must not be capable of amendment. |
| *Other standard clauses* | The trust deed will typically include, towards its end a number of standard provisions. |

# 9 The people side of moving to employee ownership; you, your employees and your leadership team

Written by Jeremy Gadd of J Gadd Associates

*"Would you tell me, please, which way I ought to go from here?"*
*"That depends a good deal on where you want to get to," said the*
*Cat.*
*"I don't much care where," said Alice.*
*"Then it doesn't matter which way you go," said the Cat.*

Lewis Carroll - Alice's Adventures in Wonderland

Carroll's famous quote is a helpful place to start this chapter. The cat's advice is worth reflecting on before you commence your journey to employee ownership.

## 9.1 Introduction

Having built up a successful business, with no doubt many hours of blood, sweat, tears and possibly the odd sleepless night, letting go is likely be an emotional experience for any owner. In the same way that airlines advise parents: *"in the event of an emergency secure your own oxygen mask before helping your children"*, a business owner contemplating a transition to employee ownership would be well advised to ensure their own thoughts and ideas about their reasons for doing so have been thoroughly worked through before they embark upon the process.

Whilst having a strong financial footing and the right legal process is essential, failure by exiting owners to understand the impact on themselves and others and to address this in a methodical and prepared way risks vastly reducing the chances of success.

This chapter deals with the *people side of employee ownership*, not under employment law, but in relation to the impact on key stakeholders. Its purpose is to help a business owner focus on what support will enable them to create a successful change.

There are many variables, so this chapter is designed to help you as owner think these through and to create your own approach. At each key decision point below, you will find some questions. These are not exhaustive, and you may have others, but they are designed to help you view the transition through a new employee ownership lens.

There is no one size fits all solution. However, there are common factors.

## 9.2 Before you start

**Question:** Every business owner should ask themselves these critical questions before they consider transitioning their business into employee ownership:

- *Why am I doing this?*
- *What do I wish to achieve?*
- *Whom will it impact outside work?*
- *What will I do afterwards? (This is very important and ties in to your first answer).*

Once you are clear on the answers, and are satisfied that you are in principle ready to divest the ownership of your business, you can then go on to consider the following regarding your business's readiness:

- *Do we have a saleable business?*
- *How central is my role to the business?*
- *Do I have a natural successor as business leader?*
- *Are the senior leadership teams great leaders or good followers?*
- *Who provides the energy which drives our business?*

Answering these further questions will allow you to develop a plan for change. This will help form your conversation with your leadership team and prepare them for the change they will need to embrace.

As previously covered in this book, there are often compelling commercial reasons for organisations to consider becoming employee-owned, with the added benefit of an attractive tax regime. However, for many, the choice feels instinctive and natural:

> *"We have always been a great place to work, where our staff are valued, encouraged and supported. Employee ownership will mean little change in how we do things".*

**Remember:** Prepare yourself first and be clear about what you would like to be doing post-transition. Make sure you are ready to let go.

**Illustration:** One CEO of a business that had become employee-owned shared their dilemma about the previous owner:

> *"Look, I really like her, and she has been an excellent support to me over the years, but it's become really difficult now. Her turning up and interfering is undermining our chances of success. I know she means well but can you help me to tell her she no longer runs this business?"*

## 9.3 Change

**Question:** What has been the most fundamental change to impact your organisation over the past five years?

If you have a good understanding of how change is experienced in your business and are ready to share that with others, this will help your leadership team members move towards both accepting and embracing this change. Change theories often make a comparison between change and bereavement. The *Kubler-Ross* change curve demonstrates the impact significant change can have on people.

Kubler-Ross change curve

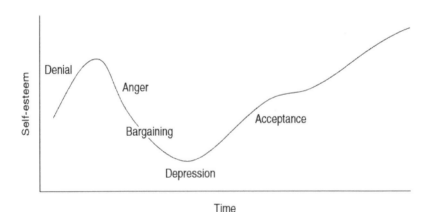

(Cameron and Green, 2015:32)

As the original owner preparing to change your role, potentially even leaving the business, you will need to be clear that your senior team is ready and able to step up and provide leadership in an employee-owned company. If you conclude that they are not, they will need training and help or, if you conclude that they will not be able to develop sufficiently even with such training, you may need to make changes.

Another big change is that the existing senior team will not just become accountable to new owners, but to new owners who in the past have been used only to answering to the leadership team. Accountability now flows in two directions: employees to leadership in relation to operations; leadership to employees in relation to company performance.

This can be an exciting prospect for some, but scary for others. They may feel that many things are changing at once. Not only is the person whom they have looked up to, reported to and relied on, signalling their eventual departure, but they now have to wrestle with the question: *"who's working for whom?"*

To them this may not feel like a simple change of ownership, but a shifting of the tectonic plates of their working life. Providing space and support through this change is another important aspect of creating a successful transition.

**Remember:** This is likely to be one of the biggest changes in your organisation's recent history. You will need to be as prepared as you can. However, you do not need all the answers, just clarity about where you are going and an understanding that it will be everyone's responsibility to make it happen.

**Illustration** – A quote from a new Director three years after their transition: "If there was an insight that the old owners shared, it was that it wasn't handed over particularly well, and I don't think it was."

## 9.4   Ownership

**Question:** It is important to understand and recognise the relationship between *"ownership"* and *"leadership"*. Ask yourself, when at work, what questions are put to you as:

- owner?
- leader?

At this point, it is worth acknowledging there is a paradox. Whilst on the face of it becoming employee-owned is just a change of ownership, in reality it is also a fundamental transition in the balance of power. On the one hand, transferring ownership is simply that other people (either directly through acquiring shares, indirectly through becoming beneficiaries of an employee trust, or sometimes both under the hybrid form of employee ownership) become the new owners. On the other hand, these new owners are likely to be the same employees who have worked for the original owner for many years. This affords great opportunity and with it brings great responsibilities for all the new employee-owners.

For many organisations the previous owners will have also been the business's leaders. They will have set the strategy, recruited and developed the team to implement it and, most importantly, have been the arbitrators in most of the important decisions (and occasionally even the unimportant ones!).

The retiring owners may no longer be able to wield such authority (and/or may not wish to). Therefore, the question of what they are going to do next is really important; not just for themselves but for the organisation itself. If you are in this position (and plan to step down from a full-time role in your company's leadership), you may have a range of choices:

- *leave and no longer have anything to do with the organisation*
- *become a trustee of the employee trust*
- *become a non-executive director of the company*
- *become a consultant*
- *or even, "return to the shop floor" and go back to working in a part of the business that you are particularly engaged by.*

Helping all involved to understand what employee ownership means for them is a fundamental building block to a successful transition. One way to bring this to life is to engage employees in a conversation about their relationship with the organisation and what the new model means in terms of their:

- *responsibilities*
- *rights*
- *opportunities.*

**Remember:** Make sure your plan is clearly understood by everyone within the organisation and if you are continuing to play a role, ensure you have a formal contract drawn up.

**Illustration:** "It became apparent one of the blockers to employees believing things had changed was that despite the owners selling their holdings to the Trust, and then becoming trustees, people saw them parking in the same reserved parking space and using the same office. To them nothing had changed!"

## 9.5 Purpose and identity

**Question:** So what do you do and who are you really?

Your organisation's purpose may well have become a part of its culture and may be at the heart of what sparked and drove you to create the business in the first place. This often forms the identity of a business. Understanding how employee ownership will further impact on its identity will be a useful part of the transition process.

It can be really helpful to capture this "purpose" in some written form. John Spedan Lewis (the founder of the John Lewis Partnership) did this by creating a formal "constitution" in 1921. To this day it guides the business through its decision-making process. Similarly, Ove Arup, the architect of employee ownership at Arup, shared his beliefs in his famous 1970 speech, which is now required reading for anyone joining Arup today. Or, more recently, David Sproxton and Peter Lord, the founders of Aardman Animations, captured their thoughts as the basis for their guiding principles, which they share at the start of the company's Partner Handbook.

Creating a constitution for some is exactly the right place to start. For others, it may feel too complicated or be unnecessary. You will decide what is best for you and your business.

## 9.6 Guiding principles

An alternative to creating a formal constitution might be to create some guiding principles, or to codify those you have already created. A useful place to start can be simply to try to capture your reflections on what drove you to create your business in the first place and what have been the common threads or beliefs that still endure. From here you, and/or others, can establish or validate guiding principles which can form part of your legacy (for example, they might be referred to in the trust deed).

Articulating the 'guiding principles' around which the organisation will be run provides a useful framework in which employee owners and leaders can hold each other to account.

**Remember:** For people to feel they can really play their part in the organisation they need to understand how to. Connecting with its values will prove fundamental in achieving this.

**Illustration:** An existing owner shared great insight with his new MD when he said to her "You'll know they understand our purpose when they can answer the question: what does employee ownership mean I can do here?"

## 9.7 Communicating the transition

**Question:** Before you share anything about your employee ownership plans you should ask yourself: *What is it I most want the team to know and how can I best help them understand this?*

When preparing your message, you will want to be able to answer:

*What is changing?*

- *Why is it changing and what were the alternatives?*
- *Over what time scale?*
- *What is known?*
- *What is not known – importantly, when will you be able to share when it is?*
- *What impact will it have on us (as the employees).*

When and how to share the message certainly requires careful consideration. There are many factors which will influence you. The size and numbers involved, whether you are seeking some kind of positive buy-in (not in a financial sense) from your leadership team and employees or simply presenting a fait accompli. However, it is recommended to consider involving staff in the following order:

- *directors and other senior leaders*
- *managers*
- *the workforce – employees, contractors, third parties*
- *clients – key ones may need particular support.*

Involving your senior leadership team in creating the transition plan, and supporting them to engage their managers, who in turn will engage their teams, will foster employee engagement in the transition. Although it may take a little longer, adopting this kind of inclusive and collegiate approach to planning employee ownership is likely to bear positive fruit.

As part of your communication, you will need to explain what is happening to the ownership of the business, why you consider employee ownership to be the best option and what the alternatives were. Be open to employee questions. It can often be helpful to present a range of frequently asked questions and answers. This should be a live document with new questions being encouraged and answered as appropriate.

Some business owners may for their own reasons prefer not to engage and involve their leadership team and employees in this way. Taking this approach may mean these questions will need to be answered after the legal transition. However, the challenge of doing so successfully is then likely to be tougher.

Be prepared. However well-intentioned your reasons, not everyone is going to like the change. As we have already explored, for some this is going to feel overwhelming.

When sharing the message:

| Do | Don't |
|---|---|
| Be clear | Over promise |
| Explain what is happening and when | Make things up |
| Share what the alternatives were | Expect everyone to welcome it |
| Share what you intend to do in the future | Treat a sale at a discounted price as a gift |
| Be open about how it will impact employees | |

**Remember:** As this will be a major change in your organisation, you will need to be as well-prepared as possible. However, you do not need all the answers, just clarity about where you are going and everyone's responsibility to make it happen.

**Illustration:** A quote from a new director soon after their transition: "With hindsight we rather rushed how we presented the ownership change to our employees and assumed they'd "get" the benefits without us taking the trouble properly to explain them, and they were underwhelmed. We're working to fix that now but it would have been better if we'd invested more time and effort earlier."

## 9.8   Engagement

**Question:** Do you have great employee engagement or good communication?

Effective communication has been a vital part in creating robust organisations for years and the importance of this for employee-owned businesses is no different. However, this is only part of establishing a highly engaging culture. Being able to explain rights, responsibilities and opportunities will prove powerful. Developing a sustainable engagement culture within an employee-owned organisation will be one of the most important building blocks to success.

There are many models and there is a range of guidance on establishing great employee engagement. In choosing the most suitable approach, it is helpful to be clear that you are engaging with employee-owners specifically, and so ensure that your approach to providing information, seeking authority for particular actions and decision-making are based on employee owners better understanding their business and supporting its continued growth and success.

**Remember:** Engagement is as much about listening as it is about telling or sharing. For this to be meaningful, everyone will need relevant and timely information.

**Illustration:** A production manager reflected: "I think it's given a slightly longer-term view of the business; I can't wait to get them (employee-owners) more involved in influencing the success of business."

## 9.9   Governance

*"The processes of interaction and decision-making among the actors involved in a collective problem that leads to the creation, reinforcement, or reproduction of social norms and institutions."*[16]

**Question:** Post transition, who should care about governance?

The answer needs to be: *everyone!*

Governance may be a dry and unexciting word but getting it right not only helps to keep an employee-owned company safe, it affords real opportunity for employee owners to participate fully in the business and to make the organisation even more successful. It helps bring to life the answers around:

- *responsibilities*
- *rights*
- *opportunities.*

Whilst governance is important, it does not need to fill everyone's working day. Good governance will reinforce a positive ownership culture. Employee owners in a successful employee-owned company will rise to the opportunity to become directly involved themselves or indirectly involved through asking questions and providing suggestions to the challenges and opportunities that face their business every day.

Participation can be through formal positions such as elected trustees, members of an Employee Council or board members, or more informal representative positions on forums or charity and leisure groups etc.

---

[16] "Investigating Policy Processes: The Governance Analytical Framework (GAF): Wiesmann, U., Hurni, H., et al.eds. Research for Sustainable Development: Foundations, Experiences, and Perspectives". Bern: *Geographica Bernensia*: 403–24.

**Remember:** Governance truly offers the opportunity for employee-owners to participate and take responsibility.

**Illustration:** When discussing governance, I was once told by the exiting joint business owner, *"We have a flat structure and do not wish to have lots of levels, this will feel very alien to us, it's not who we are"*. It was only when we explored how many roles they played as owner: leader, financier, manager and ultimate decision-maker as owner, did it become clear that even apparently flat structures have several layers of decision-making.

## 9.10 Trustees

Whilst every employee-owned company may have its own approach as to who are the trustees of its employee trust, there is often an advantage in having trustees drawn from different categories, providing a wide range of experience. The number of trustees will vary, with some companies choosing to have a representative from the board of directors (although this creates potential conflicts of interest and it is important that all trustees act in the best interests of the trust's beneficaries), an external independent trustee and also elected employee trustees. It is generally right that the trustees should evolve over time.

If there are to be one or more employee trustees, these can be introduced from the outset. Alternatively, the trustees could start without an employee trustee during the early months of the transition, while employee owners learn more about their organisation and the role of trustees, and after a period an employee trustee (or more than one) could be introduced. The employee owners can then select the most appropriate candidate to act as their elected trustee after they have become more accustomed to being owners.

## 9.11 Leadership

*"Leadership is like beauty; it's hard to define, but you know it when you see it" (Bennis, 1989:11).*

Question: Here we focus on the elements which will help you assess whether your team is equipped to lead employee-owners. Start by asking yourself:

- *Is the current team equipped with skills to lead and engage fellow employee-owners?*
- *Do they understand their own style?*
- *How comfortable are they with being questioned?*
- *Are they engaging?*
- *Are they open to change?*

It is very common for organisations to describe themselves as being 'like a family'. Eric Berne was a psychiatrist who created *Transactional Analysis* (TA) in the 1950s (Berne, 1961) as a way to explain human behaviour. He described three ego-states of individual as Parents, Adult and Child. This definition appears helpful when examining the relationship between the owner and leaders. Ideally, adult relationships will exist between the owners and the employees, particularly the leaders. However, it is quite common for many to see the owner as the parent. This means there is an organisational risk in their departing without suitable replacements in place.

For employee-owners to feel they can play an active part within their organisation, it is important that their leaders support, encourage and train them to do so. The more open, transparent and engaging they are, the greater the chances of success. Successful leaders in an employee-owned company will have the confidence and skill to share information in a way which explains and encourages others to take responsibility. This can include all but the most sensitive financial data. Creating an environment where all feel trusted and valued, believing they have the right to know and feeling they have the responsibility to act, will encourage a successful employee ownership culture.

**Remember:** In an employee-owned company, leaders will be leading people with a vested interest in their company's success. This has the potential to change the dynamic in a really positive way, with everyone pulling in the same direction.

**Illustration:** A previous owner shared "I realised I no longer had to have all the answers. This was both liberating and a little scary."

## 9.12  Creating a representative engagement body (such as an Employee Council)

**Question:**  Before establishing any arrangement to represent employees (or others) additional to an employee trust, ensure yourself of its purpose. Ask yourself: *"can I explain to any stakeholder what value this body brings?"* If not, think again.

The value of an effective representative body (such as an Employee Council) should not be underestimated. However, for it to become an effective element of an employee-owned organisation it requires the following elements:

- *a clear purpose*
- *an accountable lead, someone of seniority who can effect change*
- *organisational support*
- *relevant representation*
- *clear communication on employee owners, rights, roles and responsibilities.*

Creating an effective body requires commitment and effort from all. Whilst there are no hard and fast rules on size, organisations on one site with less than about 70 employees may well find a representative body (beyond the employee trust) unnecessary.

Once the function of the body is confirmed, establishing its 'constituencies', namely the number of representatives, length of term of office and types of election process, will all need to be carefully thought through. It can be helpful to call for volunteers from the workforce to help to establish these. Having helped to create the body, some might put themselves forward for election when required.

It may be prudent to badge the first group as a 'pilot', allowing it to trial different ways of working. These could be formal, with a Chair and minutes, or less formal with a facilitated meeting, simple bullet points and agreed next steps being recorded. Selecting a Chair or facilitator is an important decision, which should not be rushed. Try alternatives and see how they work. It is useful to agree a review timetable and criteria and share this with the trustees of the employee trust.

Before calling for an election for an Employee Council or other representative body, it is important that all within the organisation understand its role and purpose. It is worth spending time with the management and reassuring them that elected representatives do not have a veto over the normal management of the organisation.

Where managers invest time in helping representatives to carry out their role and support their understanding of the issues, there is potential for strong and productive relationships to be built.

Once the members of the body have been chosen, providing them with training and support will enable them to perform quickly as a group. This training should cover:

- *preparing for meetings*
- *gathering and sharing feedback*
- *asking questions to seek information or influence decision-making.*

**Important to remember:** Being held to account will encourage the leaders to focus on engaging all employee owners.

**Illustration:** "I realised that for the representatives on our Employee Council to support and champion the changes we needed to make, I needed to trust them, share our plans and invite their challenges. The result was a bolder more ambitious plan; it was mind-blowing".

## 9.13  Upskilling

**Question:** When you first started work, were you left to your own devices or given some form of training, support or guidance?

Whilst some may be naturally skilled at leading employee owners or even 'just' becoming an employee owner, the vast majority of us have to learn how to approach this, along with other necessary skills. As with acquiring any skill, investment will be needed to ensure all are equipped to play their part. For example, one or more employees may become elected trustees or members of a representative body, such as an Employee Council. They will need training to do this. Leadership team members are also likely to benefit from training in how to lead an employee-owned company.

Some employees' working lives, following a transition to employee ownership, may not feel too different. However, do not lose sight of the opportunities employee ownership affords to create an even better business. In order to maximise these benefits, some form of training or education around opportunities should be provided for all. It should ensure employee owners can articulate:

- *What are the responsibilities of ownership?*
- *What are the rewards of ownership?*
- *How can I and the organisation grow?*

Or more simply put their:

- *responsibilities*
- *rights*
- *opportunities.*

**Remember:** Employee ownership is simply a different form of ownership. Leveraging the advantage is a skill which requires investment.

**Illustration:** An employee-owner shared "We were always well looked after before becoming employee-owned. Afterwards, we all attended a workshop where it was explained I was now an owner, and as such much more financial information would be shared. My manager showed how costs impact on our business, these costs are our money; I have now started to shop around for our sundries and saved over £1500 in the last three months!"

# 10  The Share Incentive Plan (SIP)

Chapter 5 introduced the share incentive plan or SIP, which enables employees to claim statutory relief against income tax and National Insurance when acquiring shares in their company. This chapter considers the SIP in more detail.

## 10.1   When is a SIP relevant?

If, having established an employee trust which holds a block of shares on behalf of employees, there is a desire to create individual share ownership for all employees, the SIP is one way to approach this. Chapter 5 also looked at other ways to achieve this and these are then further considered in Chapters 11 and 14.

## 10.2   How can employees acquire shares under a SIP?

Employees can acquire shares through a SIP in the following ways, in each case with relief against income tax and National Insurance:

- *free shares*
- *the purchase of shares (called partnership shares)*
- *both free shares and share purchase*
- *share purchase with free matching shares*
- *free shares, share purchase and free matching shares*
- *dividend shares (that is, converting a taxable cash dividend into shares which would be free of income tax).*

## 10.3   Is your company eligible to establish a SIP?

A SIP may be established which provides shares in:

- *an independent private (i.e. non-publicly listed) company*
- *a company listed on recognised stock exchange*
- *a company controlled by a company listed on a recognised stock exchange (which is not a close company).*

This means that a company which is a subsidiary of another private company may not operate a SIP.

For a company which is majority-owned by an employee trust, this means that a SIP may not be available if the trust has a single corporate trustee. However, if the trust is an employee ownership trust, an exemption applies.

## 10.4 What kind of shares may be used?

Any shares used in a SIP must be ordinary shares, fully paid up and not redeemable. An ordinary share is one which is entitled to a variable rather than a fixed rate dividend.

## 10.5 Who is eligible to participate?

The SIP is an "all-employee" plan which means participation must be offered to all employees of the company on the "same terms".

Where there is a group of companies, generally all employees throughout the group must be eligible to participate.

Depending on the way in which the shares are acquired:
- *it is possible to have a qualifying period of employment*
- *the "same terms" requirement works in different ways.*

Each of these is considered later in this chapter.

## 10.6 Qualifying period of employment

Where employees are offered *free shares*, participation can be limited to employees who have been employed for up to 18 months up to the date of the award.

Where *partnership shares* are offered, participation can be limited to employees with up to 18 months' service at the date of deduction from salary, or, if there is an accumulation period, six months' service up to the date when the accumulation period begins.

## 10.7 How the SIP works

Shares allocated to employees must be held in a special SIP trust. For a company which already has an employee trust, this will be an entirely separate trust.

### (a) Establishing the SIP

To establish a SIP, a company will need to:
- *prepare rules for the SIP;*
- *prepare a SIP trust deed;*
- *decide how it wishes to offer shares (choosing from: Partnership Shares; Free Shares; Partnership and Matching Shares; Partnership Shares and Free Shares; Partnership Shares, Matching Shares and Free Shares;*

- *prepare a form of agreement setting out the terms of the share award. This could be either a free share agreement, a partnership share agreement (where matching shares are to be offered the terms will be covered by the latter agreement) or both.*

(The wording of each of these must comply with statutory requirements);

- *identify the trustees of the SIP (often there will be a single corporate trustee, which will be a subsidiary of the company);*
- *prepare an invitation to eligible employees explaining the SIP and the terms of their ownership if they decide to participate;*
- *prior to each award (and if there is an accumulation period for partnership shares, prior to the end of that period) agree the market value per share with HM Revenue and Customs;*
- *if there is an accumulation period for partnership shares, confirm to each employee the number of shares which will be awarded to them at the end of the period;*
- *keep full records of shares awarded and any changes affecting a given employee's participation; and*
- *by 6 July following the end of the tax year in which the first award was made, notify HM Revenue and Customs online about the SIP.*

## (b) Free shares

If eligible employees are to be awarded free shares, the maximum value of shares which may be awarded per employee per tax year is £3,600.

The "same terms" requirement means that:

- *every eligible employee must be awarded the same number of shares; or*
- *different employees can receive different numbers of shares provided that their allocation is based on their remuneration, length of service or hours worked (or a combination of those factors).*

It is also possible to base the determination of the number of shares to be allocated, on performance (of the company, the business unit or the individual employee). This can be done in one of two ways:

- *up to 80% of shares are performance linked, the rest on the same terms, the maximum performance linked award being no more than four times the highest same terms award;*
  or

- *all shares are performance linked, but allocation of shares within a given business unit must be on the same terms.*

A recipient of free shares must agree to retain them for a period (holding period) stipulated by the company, of at least three years but no more than five.

An award of free shares can (but does not have to) be subject to forfeiture, if the employee leaves within three years, other than for the following reasons:
- *injury or disability*
- *redundancy*
- *a relevant transfer within the meaning of the Transfer of Undertakings (Protection of Employment) Regulations 2006*
- *a change of control or other circumstances as a result of which the employee's employer is no longer an associated company of the company operating the SIP (in practice, this is most likely to mean a subsidiary is transferred out the group)*
- *retirement*
- *death.*

### (c) Partnership shares

If eligible employees are to be offered the opportunity to purchase partnership shares, those wishing to participate will agree to a regular deduction from their salary to fund the purchase of those shares. The maximum value of partnership shares per employee per tax year is £1,800 or 10% of salary, whichever is the lower.

The "same terms" requirement means that every eligible employee must be given the same opportunity to purchase partnership shares. In practice, of course, higher paid employees may be able to purchase more shares than those who are lower paid.

Shares can be purchased each time a salary deduction is made. Alternatively, it is possible to operate an accumulation period of up to one year. Where this is done, deductions from salary are made over that period, and at the end of the period shares are awarded based on how much each employee has saved. The number of shares awarded is determined by dividing the amount saved by the participant by one of the following (then rounding down to the nearest whole number):

- *the lower of the market value of a share at the beginning and end of the accumulation period and the market value of a share on the acquisition date (which cannot be more than 30 days after the end of the accumulation period);*
- *the market value of a share at the beginning of the accumulation period; or*
- *the market value of a share on the acquisition date.*

The participant's partnership share agreement must specify which of these methods will be used.

If a participant leaves during an accumulation period, the partnership share money that they have saved must be returned to them. If they leave after the end of an accumulation period but before the acquisition date, the shares should be awarded to them but those shares will then immediately cease to be subject to the plan.

### (d) Matching shares

*Matching shares* are also free shares, the number awarded to each employee being linked to the number of partnership shares awarded. The maximum ratio of matching to partnership shares is 2:1 but subject to that each company can (if it wishes to award matching shares) set its own ratio.

As with free shares, there must be a holding period of between three and five years. By offering matching shares, a company can in effect enable employees to purchase shares at a discount to their market value. For example, one matching share for every two partnership shares means the effective purchase price per share overall reduces by a third.

### (e) Dividend shares

If dividends are paid on shares awarded under a SIP, it is possible to allow the dividends to be paid in the form of additional shares, rather than cash. Unlike with cash dividends, these additional *dividend shares* do not give rise to an income tax liability, as long as they are retained for three years.

It is not a requirement to offer dividend shares. Where they do feature, the SIP rules can allow each participant to choose whether they take their dividends as cash or shares or it can be made compulsory for them to take the dividends as shares.

## 10.8 How the tax reliefs work

### (a) Partnership shares

If an employee purchases partnership shares by deduction from their pay, they benefit from relief against income tax and National Insurance on the amount deducted.

For example, if an employee agrees to a deduction of £50 per month to fund the purchase of partnership shares, £50 will go directly towards the purchase of shares, with no tax being deducted. There will also be no requirement for the employer to pay employer's National Insurance on that amount.

The maximum annual value per employee of partnership shares which can be awarded is £1,800.

For the employee to claim the relief, the shares must normally then be retained for a five year period.

If a participant withdraws their shares earlier (leaving will automatically mean the shares are treated as withdrawn), income tax and National Insurance will become payable after all. The tax calculation will depend upon how long the shares have been held:

- *if less than three years, tax is due on the shares' value at the date of withdrawal; or*
- *if between three and five years, tax is due on the lower of the amount of the participant's pay used to acquire the shares and the shares' market value on the date of withdrawal from the SIP.*

The tax due must be collected and paid under PAYE.

However, there are exceptions, where no tax liability arises:

- *the participant leaves due to injury or disability, redundancy, TUPE transfer, retirement, death or their company ceasing to be an associated company; or*

- *a cash takeover of the Company[17] where there is no possibility of being paid in shares.*

## (b) Free and matching shares

Where an employee is given free or matching shares, they will not be subject to income tax or National Insurance at the time of the award.

The maximum annual value per employee of free shares which can be awarded is £3,600. The same limit applies to matching shares because the maximum ratio of matching to partnership shares is 2:1 and the maximum annual value of partnership shares per employee is £1,800.

As with partnership shares, a key condition of this tax relief is that the shares must normally be held for a five year period.

If a participant withdraws them earlier (including on leaving, as with partnership shares), income tax and National Insurance becomes payable. The tax calculation will depend on how long the shares have been held:

- *if less than three years, tax is due on the shares' value at the date of withdrawal; or*
- *if between three and five years, tax is due on the lower of market value on the date when the shares were first awarded and on the date of withdrawal from the SIP.*

The tax due must be collected and paid under PAYE.

However, there are exceptions, where no tax liability arises:

- *the participant leaves due to injury or disability, redundancy, TUPE transfer, retirement, death or their company ceasing to be an associated company; or*
- *a cash takeover of the Company where there is no possibility of being paid in shares.*

---

[17] This is quite narrowly defined as being under a court-sanctioned scheme of arrangement, a change of control by general offer or operation of the Companies Act minority "squeeze out" provisions. It may not therefore necessarily apply where a change of control takes place under a contract between seller(s) and buyer.

### (c) Dividend shares

Where an employee takes dividend shares in place of a cash dividend, there is no income tax liability on the shares' value.

A key condition is that the dividend shares must be left in the SIP for three years. If taken out earlier, income tax is due at the dividend rate.

However, if shares are withdrawn from the plan within three years on a cash takeover (see above), there is no income tax liability.

### (d) Disposals of SIP shares

Where shares that have been awarded to an employee under a SIP are disposed of, there is no CGT on any gain.

## 10.9 The need to agree market value with HM Revenue and Customs

Prior to each award of shares under a SIP, it is a requirement to agree share valuation with HM Revenue and Customs.

For the purposes of any share awards under a SIP, market value means the unrestricted market value of a share. In other words, it is necessary to disregard the impact on a share's value of any restrictions affecting it which may otherwise reduce its value (for example, restrictions on the ability to transfer it or an obligation to offer it for sale in certain circumstances).

Any valuation agreed for a SIP award will normally be valid for six months, although if a significant event happens during that period which may impact on value (such as a transaction in shares which suggests a higher value per share compared with that agreed with HM Revenue and Customs), it is necessary to re-apply.

Where partnership shares are awarded under an accumulation period (see 10.7) it will be necessary to agree a valuation both at the beginning and end of the period unless the accumulation period is less than six months, in which case the valuation agreed at the start of the period may continue to apply at the end.

## 10.10  A trap to avoid: disqualifying events

The SIP tax reliefs will cease to be available for any new share awards (although existing awards will not be affected) upon the occurrence of these *disqualifying events*:

- *any alteration to the company's share capital, or to the rights attaching to shares, which materially affects the value of shares awarded under the SIP; or*
- *SIP shares receiving different treatment compared with other shares of the same class, regarding dividends, capital repayments, rights issues or other offers of additional shares or securities.*

## 10.11  Using a SIP to award shares held in an employee ownership trust

Where an employee ownership trust permits transfers of shares to individual employees (always ensuring that the trust retains more than 50% of the shares) it might be reasonable to expect this to be done through a SIP, enabling employees to benefit from the income tax and National Insurance reliefs. Both the SIP and the employee ownership trust contain very similar requirements regarding "same terms".

In practice, this is not always straightforward and whether it is possible is likely to depend upon how shares are to be awarded.

An employee ownership trust can (as long as the trust deed contains the necessary powers) sell shares at market value to a SIP trust, after which the SIP trust can offer those shares to employees as partnership shares, free shares or matching shares.

The following issues can arise:

- *where shares are awarded under the SIP as free shares, the SIP trust will clearly receive no funds from employees to cover the purchase price it has paid to the employee ownership trust, so it is likely that this will need to be paid by the company;*
- *to avoid this problem, the employee ownership trust may be able to gift shares directly to employees to be held under the SIP;*
- *where shares are awarded under the SIP as partnership shares with an accumulation period, there may also be complications, as it will not be known how many shares are to be awarded until the end of the period.*

*The employee ownership trust may not sell its shares at any time for less than their market value. It could sell sufficient shares to the SIP at the beginning of the period to satisfy awards assuming no change in value, paid for using a loan from the company.[18] If share value rose during the accumulation period, the SIP would have sufficient shares, but if it fell, the SIP would then need to source additional shares from the employee ownership trust, paying the market value price at that time. In the latter case it would require top up funding from the company to cover the purchase price of these additional shares; and*

• *if the employee ownership trust's share sale crystallises a capital gain, it will be liable for CGT on that gain.*

Given that it may be necessary to navigate a complex path if shares in an employee ownership trust are to be allocated to employees through a SIP, it may often be preferable for the company itself to issue new shares to satisfy SIP awards. The number of shares held by the EOT will not diminish although the size of its holding as a percentage will do.

## 10.12  Taxation of SIP trustees

Where the SIP trustees receive dividends on shares that have not yet been awarded to employees, they will not be subject to income tax as long as the shares are awarded within two years of acquisition. However, that period will increase to five years if the shares are not "readily convertible assets" (in other words, listed shares or shares for which there is a market enabling them to be converted into cash).

In relation to disposals of shares by the SIP, provided that the SIP trustees award shares they hold to employees within two years of acquisition, any growth in value between acquisition and award to employees will also be exempt from CGT in the hands of the SIP trustees.

---

[18] Any loan from a company which is a close company, to a SIP trust is likely to be regarded as a loan to a participator (Corporation Tax Act 2010, section 455) triggering a tax liability on the company of 32.5% of the loan if it remains unpaid at the end of the company's financial period. The tax is refunded if the loan is repaid.

A purchase of existing issued shares by SIP trustees will be subject to stamp duty. If shares are gifted to the SIP trustees or they subscribe for new shares, no stamp duty will be payable in either of those circumstances.

Any subsequent award or transfer of shares to a SIP participant will not be subject to stamp duty.

## 10.13  Tax-deductibility of SIP costs

A company is allowed a corporation tax deduction for:

- *the expenses incurred in establishing a SIP;*
- *payments by the company to the SIP's trustees to cover: interest on loans taken out by trustees to fund share acquisition; commissions or fees; stamp duty and other incidental costs; and*
- *other expenses of an income nature which it incurs in operating the SIP.*

There are three additional circumstances where a corporation tax deduction is available.

The first may arise where partnership shares have been offered under an accumulation period and additional shares are required at the end of the period because (a) the SIP trust is to acquire its shares at the end of the period, (b) share value has risen over the period, (c) the participant is entitled to be awarded shares at market value as at the beginning of the period (or the lower of market value at the beginning and end), resulting in (d) the SIP trust having insufficient shares. In this situation, the cost to the company of funding the SIP trust to acquire additional shares is corporation tax deductible.

The second relates to awards of free and matching shares. The company may claim a corporation tax deduction for an amount equal to the value of those shares when awarded to a participant.

Under the third, the company may claim corporation tax relief if:

- *it funds a SIP trust to acquire shares (in the funding company or its holding company);*
- *the trustees of the SIP use that money for that purpose, but do not acquire them from a company;*

- *twelve months after those shares were acquired, the SIP trustees hold at least 10% of the ordinary share capital in the company whose shares they acquired (and are also entitled to at least 10% of profits available for distribution and assets on a liquidation); and*
- *30% or more of the shares acquired must have been awarded by the SIP to employees within five years and all of them must have been awarded within ten years. This is given effect by allowing the deduction for the accounting period in which the twelve month period referred to above ends but then withdrawing it if these conditions are not met, although the deduction is reinstated if all the shares are subsequently awarded to employees.)*

This deduction was introduced in 2003 (under the Employee Share Schemes Act 2002) following an earlier attempt to foster wider employee share ownership.

## 10.14   CGT relief on selling to a SIP

A precursor to the CGT relief on selling to an employee ownership trust, which is understood not to be widely used, is the ability to defer CGT on transferring shares to a SIP.

This was also introduced by the Employee Share Schemes Act 2002. It is not understood to have been used significantly and the introduction of the employee ownership trust in 2014 is likely to mean that it will be of limited application.

The main conditions are:
- *the transferring shareholder must not be a company;*
- *the shares must be in a company that is not controlled by another company;*
- *the sale proceeds must be reinvested in other chargeable assets (replacement assets) within six months of the date when the SIP has a 10% holding (see below); and*
- *the SIP must hold at least 10% of the company's ordinary share capital (and be entitled to at least 10% of profits available for distribution and assets on a liquidation).*

The relief allows a deferral of CGT but it is not eliminated. A condition of the CGT deferral is that sale proceeds are reinvested. The transferor is treated as having disposed of the shares for a consideration giving rise neither to a gain nor a loss, the amount paid for the replacement chargeable assets being deemed to be reduced by the excess over that "no gain or loss" consideration. In effect, the capital gain on the shares is rolled over into the replacement assets, so that when they are disposed of, the original CGT liability will come back to life.

## 10.15 Notifications to HM Revenue and Customs

- By 6 July following the end of the tax year in which a first award of shares under a SIP is made, HM Revenue and Customs must be notified of the SIP's establishment, using their online service.
- Subsequently, during the life of the SIP, an annual return must be filed annually, by 6 July.

**To recap:**
- Under a SIP, employees can buy shares with income tax relief (partnership shares) and/or receive free shares income tax free.
- Free shares can be offered, to match shares bought (matching shares).
- There is no National Insurance.
- A SIP is for all employees who must be offered shares on the same terms (although a qualifying period of up to 18 months is allowed).
- Not all companies are eligible to operate a SIP and it is important to check the conditions.
- Shares must normally be held for five years but can be withdrawn earlier without loss of tax relief if the employee leaves for certain "good leaver" reasons or there is a cash takeover of the company.
- Prior to each award of shares, share value must be agreed with HMRC.
- It may be complex to award shares held in an employee ownership trust through a SIP.
- Registration with HMRC is required.

# 11 Save As You Earn (SAYE) options

## 11.1 Introduction

SAYE options can be used as a way of involving all of a company's employees in its ownership. As Chapter 5 has explained, an SAYE option plan offers a tax advantage to participating employees (growth in value of the shares under option is taxed as capital gain, not income), conditional on all employees with the minimum qualifying period of employment being invited to participate.

Whilst SAYE options may have a role to play in a company wishing to introduce individual employee share ownership, it is difficult to see how they could be deployed to transfer shares out of an employee ownership trust. Because it is *unlikely* that all employees eligible to receive shares from a company's employee ownership trust will wish to participate, and in turn *likely* that some of those who do participate will drop out during the option period, by the time it comes to transferring shares to participants (at the end of the option period) invariably not all employees who are beneficiaries of the employee ownership trust will acquire shares from it, and so it is would be difficult to satisfy the all-employee requirement. Further, employees who do participate will choose to save different amounts towards their option exercise price and will therefore be granted different numbers of options, so it is unlikely the "same terms" conditions for employee ownership trusts could be met either.

There is no reason why SAYE options could not be granted by the company itself over new issue shares, by another shareholder or by an employee benefit trust.

## 11.2 How do SAYE options work?

"Save as you earn" is a an "all-employee" share scheme, which means that the opportunity to participate must be offered to all employees of a company (or group of companies) who have completed a qualifying period of employment (see 9.5), on similar terms.

The option exercise price may be market value at the date of grant, greater than market value (unusual) or discounted from market value by up to 20%. Where SAYE options are granted by a private company, market value must be agreed with HM Revenue and Customs in advance. "Market value" means a share's unrestricted market value; in other words it does not allow for any discount to reflect the valuation impact of restrictions on the shares over which options are to be granted.

Each employee wishing to be granted SAYE options must agree to save a fixed amount per month, by deduction from their pay, over a time period of three or five years. At the same time, they are granted an option to acquire shares, the total exercise price of which is the same as the total savings they will make (including interest[19]) over their savings period.

At the end of the savings period (in fact, within up to six months of the end), the optionholder will decide whether to exercise their option (or to do so in part) or simply to withdraw their savings.

### Case study: Eamont Engineering Limited

### *Using SAYE options to create individual employee share ownership*
Eamont Engineering is 75% owned by an employee ownership trust, the remaining 25% being held by the company's original founding shareholder, Jane Eamont. It has 95 employees, of whom 70 have been with the company for more than two years.

The company's directors, with the support of the trustees, want employees to have the opportunity to acquire shares and have chosen SAYE options as their preferred route. They like the fact that employees do not have to commit to purchasing shares until the end of a three or five year option period, at which time they can decide either to (a)

---

[19] At the time of writing, no interest is paid under SAYE savings contracts. Should circumstances change and interest again be paid, this will be a fixed rate known at the beginning of the savings contract, the amount of which will be taken into account in determining what will be the optionholder's total savings by the end of the period and so the number of options to be granted. Any such interest is income tax free and is commonly referred to as a "tax free bonus".

exercise their options using the money they have saved or (b) let their options lapse and keep their savings.

SAYE options are offered by the company to the 70 employees who have two years' service.

It is agreed with HMRC that each share is worth £1. The company is willing to discount the option exercise price by the maximum 20% allowed, making the exercise price 80p per share.

Taking one employee as an example, Gervase agrees to save £100 per month over a three year period. Currently his savings won't receive any interest, so at the end of the savings period he will have £3,600, which will buy him 4,500 shares at the 80p per share exercise price.

Three years later, each share is worth £2. Gervase decides to exercise his option, paying £3,600 for shares now worth £9,000. He will not have to pay income tax or National Insurance on his gain.

After a further five years, each share is now worth £5, so Gervase's total holding is now valued at £22,500. If he then sells his shares (assuming there is a buyer) for market value, he will make a capital gain of £18,900 (£22,500 - £3,600), upon which he will pay CGT.

### Impact on the company's total shareholdings
If all options are exercised, the company will need to issue new shares comprising 7.5% of the company's total issued shares. This will mean that the percentage shareholdings are then:
EOT – 69.5%
Jane – 23.1%
Employees – 7.4%

The EOT and Jane are willing to accept this percentage dilution on the basis that it will benefit the company overall to have individual employee shareholders. Critically, the EOT's holding remains over more than 50% of the shares, ensuring that there is no clawback of the CGT relief claimed by Jane when she sold her shares to the EOT and that the company continues to be able to pay bonuses to employees income tax free.

## 11.3  Is your company eligible?
SAYE options may be granted over shares in a company which is:
* *an independent private (i.e. non-publicly listed) company*
* *a company listed on recognised stock exchange*
* *a company controlled by a company listed on a recognised stock exchange (which is not a close company).*

This means that SAYE options may not be granted over shares in a company which is subsidiary of another private company.

For a company which is majority-owned by an employee trust, this means that SAYE options may not be available if the trust has a single corporate trustee. However, if the trust is an employee ownership trust, an exemption applies.

## 11.4 What kind of shares may be used?

Any shares used in an SAYE option scheme must be ordinary shares, fully paid up and not redeemable. An ordinary share is one which is entitled to a variable rather than a fixed rate dividend.

In addition, if the company whose shares are to be the subject of SAYE options has more than one class of share, there is an additional requirement whose purpose is to prevent the creation of a special (inferior) class of "employee shares". Under this requirement, the majority of the issued shares of the same class as those over which the options are to be granted must either be *employee-control shares* or *open market shares*.

| | Employee control shares | Open market shares |
|---|---|---|
| Purpose and overview | If satisfied, this test shows that a majority of the shares of the same class give employees control of the company and so are not to be regarded as inferior to shares of any other class | If satisfied, this test shows that a majority of the shares of the same class are held by persons other than employees or directors, and so are shares which can be regarded as ones which investors have committed to holding |
| Conditions | Shares are "employee-control" shares if:<br>• those shares give the persons holding them control of the company and<br>• those persons are or have been employees or directors of the company or another company which controls the company | A majority of the shares must be held by persons other than (for an independent private company):<br>• those who acquired them as directors or employees and not under a public share offer and<br>• trustees holding shares on behalf of the above (this would include SIP trustees in relation to shares |

| | | allocated to employees but not in relation to any non-allocated shares, and would not include shares in an employee benefit trust or employee ownership trust which have not been allocated to particular employees) |
|---|---|---|

## 11.5  Who is eligible to participate?

SAYE options is an "all-employee" plan which means participation must be offered to all employees with a minimum period of employment on "similar terms".

Where the company is part of a group of companies, all employees throughout the group must generally be eligible to participate.

## 11.6  Qualifying period of employment

The company may (but does not have to) stipulate that if an employee is to be granted SAYE options they must have completed a qualifying period of employment, which can be set at up to five years.

## 11.7  Similar terms

When setting the level of participation per employee, it is possible to set different levels of participation (by reference to the amount of monthly saving/maximum number of options or length of savings period) provided this is done according to remuneration, length of service or similar factors.

In practice, all eligible employees are likely to be given the same opportunity to participate, although higher paid employees may save a greater amount each month.

An SAYE option scheme must not contain features which would discourage any eligible employee from participating. Where there is a group of companies, the scheme must not operate in a way which confers benefit wholly or mainly on directors or the most highly paid employees in the group.

## 11.8 Limits

There is a maximum total savings amount per employee, depending on the length of the savings period (in each case, this equates to £500 per month):

- *three year savings period: £18,000*
- *five year savings period: £30,000.*

The minimum monthly saving amount per employee is £5.

The rules of an SAYE option scheme can provide for scaling down, so that if employees in aggregate save an amount which would purchase more shares than are available, the amount of each employee's savings can be reduced. This must be done on a "fair and reasonable" basis, and is often done on the basis that all applications will be scaled down pro rata until the aggregate savings match the number of available shares. Alternatively (recognising that this approach works in favour of those who can afford to save more), it is possible to limit scaling down to those employees who have applied to save a monthly amount greater than a specified amount.

## 11.9 Leavers

An SAYE option must provide the following, to cover different situations where an optionholder ceases to be an employee. In each case the right of exercise is limited to the amount saved up to the date falling six months after leaving:

| Reason for leaving | Right of optionholder |
|---|---|
| Death | Option may be exercised by personal representatives within 12 months of death (otherwise it will lapse) |
| Injury, disability, redundancy | Option may be exercised within six months (otherwise it will lapse) |
| Retirement | Option may be exercised within six months (otherwise it will lapse) |
| TUPE transfer or change of control of associated company employing optionholder | Option may be exercised within six months (otherwise it will lapse) |
| Leaving for any other reason within three years of the date of option grant | Option lapses |

The scheme rules may also provide that if an optionholder leaves more than three years after the option grant, the option may be exercised within six months, or the rules may say that exercise is permitted in certain circumstances, depending on the reason for leaving. There is no requirement, however, to allow exercise, other than as is provided for in the above table.

The rules may not provide for directors to have discretion as to whether an SAYE option can be exercised.

## 11.10 When income tax is payable

If the scheme rules allow an optionholder to exercise their options early (less than three years after the option grant) on a takeover (apart from certain situations – see below), then their option gain (the difference between option exercise price and market value at the date of option exercise) will be subject to income tax (and, if the shares are readily convertible assets, National Insurance).

An SAYE option may however be exercised within three years without income tax being payable, if the company is taken over for cash and the takeover is structured as a general offer, a court-sanctioned scheme of arrangement, a non-UK reorganisation arrangement or under the compulsory "squeeze out" provisions in the Companies Act 2006. The option must be exercised within six months.

Where an SAYE optionholder exercises their option within three years of the grant due to death or leaving employment by reason of disability, injury, redundancy, retirement, a TUPE transfer or the optionholder's employer company ceasing to be an associated company, there will be no income tax liability. The option must, however, be exercised within six months (or 12 months in the case of death).

## 11.11 Agreeing market value with HM Revenue and Customs

Unless the shares over which SAYE options are to be granted are quoted on a recognised stock exchange, their market value must be agreed in advance of the option grant with HM Revenue and Customs.

## (a) Corporation tax

The employing company will be able to claim relief against corporation tax in respect of option gains, subject to meeting the conditions (see Chapter 19).

The expenses of establishing an SAYE option scheme are deductible for corporation tax purposes.

## 11.12  Establishing an SAYE option scheme

The key steps to establish an SAYE option scheme are:

- *confirm that the eligibility conditions are satisfied and whether a qualifying period of employment is to apply;*
- *prepare rules of the SAYE scheme which meet the statutory requirements;*
- *plan for how shares acquired by participants may eventually be sold;*
- *establish a savings arrangement with a bank or building society that is HM Revenue and Customs certified;*
- *agree market value with HM Revenue and Customs;*
- *prepare an invitation to eligible employees explaining how SAYE options work and what the terms of their options will be if they decide to participate, with an application form and savings contract for participation;*
- *receive applications to participate and completed savings contracts;*
- *issue option certificates to participating employees;*
- *initiate monthly salary deductions (out of net pay) and pay these to the savings provider;*
- *keep full records of options and any changes affecting a given employee's participation, for example, their leaving; and*
- *notify HM Revenue and Customs online about the SAYE scheme (see below).*

A procedure must be followed at the end of the savings period, under which participants either exercise their options using their savings or simply withdraw those savings. To assist participants in making a decision, a private company operating an SAYE option scheme may consider commissioning an independent share valuation, demonstrating whether and if so, to what extent, value per share at the time when the options become exercisable is greater than the exercise price.

## 11.13   Notifications to HM Revenue and Customs

- By 6 July following the end of the tax year in which a first grant of options under an SAYE option scheme was made, HM Revenue and Customs must be notified of the SIP's establishment, using their online service.
- Subsequently, during the life of the SAYE scheme an annual return must be filed annually, by 6 July.

**To recap:**

- SAYE options must be offered to all employees (although a qualifying period of employment of up to five years is allowed) on similar terms.
- If a company that is controlled by an employee ownership trust wishes to grant SAYE options, it is recommended that this be over new issue shares rather than shares in the EOT.
- Not all companies are eligible to operate an SAYE option scheme and it is important to check the conditions.
- Employees who agree to participate must commit to saving a fixed regular amount from their salary which will, after the option period (three or five years), fund the exercise of their option if they wish to exercise.
- There is no obligation to exercise the option at the end of the option period. The employee can choose instead to keep the money saved.
- For any private company granting SAYE options, market value must be agreed in advance with HMRC.
- Option gains are not subject to income tax or National Insurance. Instead, CGT is charged when the shares are eventually sold. Normally at least three years must pass before the option can be exercised income tax free but in certain circumstances it may be exercised earlier free of income tax.
- Income tax relief is not given for money saved under SAYE options.
- Registration with HMRC is required.

# 12 EMI options

## 12.1 Introduction

Chapter 5 gave an overview of EMI options. This chapter goes into more detail and will assist a company which is contemplating using EMI options as a way for its key employees to become shareholders, to:

- *Evaluate whether this is the right approach;*
- *Confirm whether the company is eligible to grant EMI options; and*
- *Understand the principal steps in creating and then operating an EMI option scheme.*

## 12.2 When EMI options may be suitable

A company which has become majority employee-owned (whether by an employee ownership trust, an employee benefit trust, a hybrid of trust and individual share ownership or (unusually, perhaps other than in a co-operative) by employees holding shares personally with no separate trust, may wish to introduce a separate share ownership arrangement for its key people.

Those participating, typically directors and sometimes other members of the senior leadership team, would be granted rights to acquire a greater number of shares than non-management employees. It would not be possible to use a SIP or SAYE option scheme, as each of these must involve all employees on the same/similar terms.

The company will therefore need to look at other approaches, under which participation can be limited to chosen employees. If they require to minimise the tax which participants must pay, it makes sense to begin by looking at EMI options.

## 12.3 How do EMI options work?

In brief, a chosen participant is granted an option to acquire a specified number of shares in their employer company (or its holding company) at a fixed exercise price.

An EMI option is typically capable of being exercised after a period of time or on a certain event. The terms of the option may phase in when the option can be exercised (for example, 25% after one year, then the balance over the following three years in quarterly instalments) and will often provide that if the optionholder leaves they will either lose their option or they will do so if they leave in certain "bad leaver" circumstances.

The key tax benefit of EMI options are:

- *an EMI option can be structured so that (unlike with a non-approved option) no income tax or National Insurance is payable when the option is exercised;*[20] *and*
- *tax only becomes due when, following the exercise of the option, the shares are eventually sold, at which point the tax due is CGT.*

See also Chapter 5.

## 12.4    Is your company eligible?

EMI options are available for smaller, independent companies who carry on permitted businesses.

The qualifying conditions are considered below.

### (a)  Size of company

A company wishing to grant EMI options must not have:

- *gross assets of £30 million or more; or*
- *250 or more full-time employees.*

Both these requirements must be satisfied. It is important not to refer to *net assets* when considering the first test.

Under the second test, a company which has 250 employees or more would still be eligible if in aggregate the number of full-time employees was less than 250, pro-rating part-time employees based on hours worked. For example, a company with 100 full-time employees and 200 working three days per week would pass the test (100 + 3/5 of 200 = 220 full-time equivalent employees).

---

[20] This is done by making the option exercise price at least the same as market value at the date when the option is granted. If exercise price is less than market value on grant, income tax (and possibly also National Insurance) will be payable on exercise, on the difference between the two (in other words, on the discount from market value at the date of grant).

Each of these tests is only measured at the date when EMI options are granted. If subsequent company growth results in either test ceasing to be satisfied, that will not affect EMI options already granted but will prevent the grant of further EMI options.

## (b) Independence

If EMI options are to be granted over shares in a private company, it must be an independent company. This means that it must not be a 51% subsidiary of any other company, or otherwise under the control of another company or another company plus any person *connected* with it.

A company which is under the control of an employee ownership trust is treated as satisfying the independence requirement, including where it has a corporate trustee.

Additionally, there must be no arrangements in place under which the company could become a subsidiary or controlled by another company.

### (i) Joint ventures

Special care is needed where the company is a joint venture vehicle. This is because its shareholders may be regarded as connected with each other (on the basis that they have signed a detailed agreement governing how they are together going to operate the joint venture), which means that although no single company may hold more than 50% of the company, each corporate shareholder will be regarded as doing so, and the independence test will not be met.

Where the company itself holds shares in another company as part of a joint venture with one or more other shareholders, it may not qualify to grant EMI options. The company in which the shares are held will be regarded as a subsidiary (because of the connections rule), but will not be a *qualifying subsidiary.* The EMI legislation requires any subsidiary of a company wishing to grant options to be owned as to at least 51% by that company.

### (ii) What does control mean?

A company will have control of another company if the first company can secure that the affairs of the second company are conducted in accordance with its wishes:

- *by means of its shareholding or voting power; or*
- *as a result of any powers conferred by the articles of association or other document regulating the second company.*

The first of these tests involves control at shareholder level, the second involves control at board level. If a company is able to decide who the directors of another company should be, it is likely that it will be regarded as controlling that company.

Reserving consent rights to a particular shareholder is not on its own likely to result in that shareholder having control.

## (c) Qualifying subsidiaries

If the company controls any other company (on its own or with a connected person):

- *the controlling company must own more than 50% of the subsidiary's ordinary share capital;*
- *the subsidiary must not be under the control of any person other than the controlling company or another of its subsidiaries; and*
- *there must be no arrangements under which either of the conditions above would cease to be met.*

Controlled companies that meet these requirements are *qualifying subsidiaries*.

## (d) Permanent UK establishment

One of these tests must be satisfied:

*The company must have a UK permanent establishment; or*

If it does not have a UK permanent establishment but is a parent company, any other member of its group must:

- *either be carrying on a qualifying trade (see below) or be preparing to do so; and*
- *have a UK permanent establishment.*

A company will be regarded as having a permanent UK establishment if:

- *it has a fixed UK place of business through which its business is wholly or partly carried on. This includes a place of management; a branch; an office; a factory; a workshop; an installation or structure for the exploration of natural resources; a mine; an oil or gas well; a quarry or any other place of extraction of natural resources; or a building site or construction or installation project; or*

- *an agent acting for the company has, and habitually exercises in the UK, authority to do business on the company's behalf and that agent is not of independent status acting in the ordinary course of its business.*

## (e) Qualifying trade

The policy behind the EMI tax legislation is to provide incentives for employees of entrepreneurial and/or scalable businesses. For this reason, a company wishing to grant EMI options must exist to carry on a "qualifying trade" and be either carrying on such a trade or preparing to do so.

A qualifying trade:

- *must be undertaken on a commercial basis with a view to making profits; and*
- *must not, to a substantial extent, consist of certain excluded activities.*

## (i) Excluded activities

Each of the following is an excluded activity:

- *dealing in land, commodities or futures, or shares, securities or other financial instruments*
- *dealing in goods, otherwise than in the course of an ordinary trade of wholesale or retail distribution*
- *banking, insurance, money-lending, debt-factoring, hire purchase financing or other financial activities*
- *leasing (including letting ships on charter, or other assets on hire) or receiving royalties or other licence fees*
- *providing legal or accountancy services*
- *property development*
- *farming or market gardening*
- *holding, managing or occupying woodlands or any other forestry activities or timber production*
- *operating or managing hotels or comparable establishments, such as a guest house or hostel, or managing property used as a hotel or comparable establishment*
- *operating or managing nursing homes or residential care homes, or managing property used as a nursing home or residential care home*

- *providing services or facilities for a business carried on by another person if:*
  - *the business consists, to a substantial extent, of excluded activities; and*
  - *a controlling interest in the business is held by a person who also has a controlling interest in the business carried on by the company providing the services or facilities*
- *shipbuilding*
- *coal production*
- *steel production.*

HM Revenue and Customs guidance is that activities comprising more than 20% of a company's trade are to be regarded as substantial.

## 12.5 Which employees can be granted EMI options?

An EMI option may only be granted to an employee if the following requirements are met:

- *they must be an employee of the company whose shares are subject to the options, or of a qualifying subsidiary;*
- *they must be full-time (that is, they must work for that company at least 25 hours a week, or otherwise at least 75% of their total working time);*
- *they must not already hold 30% of the company's shares (including any shares held by their business partner, spouse, civil partner, parents, children, other relatives in the direct line and certain trusts); and*
- *they must not be a director who is not also an employee.*

## 12.6 Over what kinds of share can EMI options be granted?

EMI options must be granted over ordinary shares which are fully paid up and not redeemable. It is possible to have more than one class of ordinary shares and to grant options over one of those classes of ordinary shares.

### (a) Ordinary shares

Ordinary share capital means all the issued share capital (by whatever name called) of the company, other than capital which carries a right to a fixed rate dividend and no other right to share in the profits of the company.

HM Revenue and Customs will treat as ordinary share capital shares which have no rights to receive dividends and shares which have a right to the greater of a specified sum or to the dividend paid in respect of another class of share.

### (b) Fully paid up

Fully paid up means that the subscription price for the shares is paid before the shares are issued. Shares issued without full payment of at least their nominal value will not be fully paid.

If EMI options are to be granted over shares already issued, it will be necessary to check that at least the nominal value of those shares has been paid up at the time of option grant.

If EMI options are to be granted over newly issued shares (that is, new shares will be issued when the option is exercised), the option exercise price must be at least nominal value and must be paid on exercise.

### (c) Not redeemable

A share is redeemable if it is to be redeemed by the company or liable to be redeemed at the option of the company or its holder.

### (d) Granting options over a separate class of ordinary share

A separate class of shares can be created to be used for grants of EMI options. For example, these shares could:

- *be non-voting*
- *be non-dividend bearing*
- *have different rights to return of capital on a sale or liquidation.*

## 12.7    Purpose of EMI options

An EMI option grant must be granted "for commercial reasons in order to recruit or retain an employee in a company, and not as part of a scheme or arrangement the main purpose (or one of the main purposes) of which is the avoidance of tax".

## 12.8 Financial limits

No employee may hold EMI options over shares which have (measured at the date of grant) an aggregate value greater than £250,000.

This limit does not apply to any growth in value of option shares following grant.

If an EMI optionholder also holds CSOP options (see Chapter 13), the value of those options is taken into account.

There is also an aggregate limit for all outstanding options, of £3 million. The aggregation works in the same way.

Each of these limits is based on the unrestricted market value of shares.

Options granted in excess of these financial limits will be treated as non-approved options without tax advantages.

### The EMI £250,000 limit: an example

Howgill Energy Limited grants options to Andrea Kirkby to acquire 30,000 ordinary shares, each with a market value of £5. The aggregate value of her option shares is £150,000.

Two years later, Andrea receives a further option grant over 10,000 shares, each share now having a value of £8. She has not exercised any of her original options.

The aggregate value of her option shares is £230,000:

- 30,000 x £5; and
- 10,000 x £8

### Total = £230,000

## 12.9 Taxation of the optionholder

The taxation of EMI options will depend on whether the option exercise price is set at (a) market value or above or (b) below market value and on whether (c) an EMI disqualifying event occurs between option grant and exercise.

### (a) Exercise price set at or above market value

If the option exercise price per share is set at or above market value at the date of the option grant:

- *no tax will be due on the grant of the option;*
- *no tax will be due on the exercise of the option (unless there has been a disqualifying event between grant and exercise – see below);*
- *capital gains tax will be due on the eventual sale of the shares, on growth in value from the date of the option grant.*

### Alston Intelligence Limited: EMI options granted with a market value exercise price

#### Grant of options
The market value of an ordinary share in Alston Intelligence Limited has been agreed with HM Revenue and Customs to be £3 (before taking into account the impact of restrictions on the shares). The shares are subject to one main restriction, under which any shareholder wishing to sell must offer them for sale internally. HM Revenue and Customs agree that this reduces value to £2.50.

The £3 value is called unrestricted market value and the £2.50 value is called actual market value.

Options are granted to Mo Stanhope, who recently joined the company, over 10,000 shares with an exercise price of £2.50 per share.

#### Exercise of the options
Three years later, Mo exercises his options. Each share is now worth £5. He pays £2.50 per share and no tax.

#### Sale of the shares
After a further five years, Mo sells his shares for £10 each. He has made a total gain of £75,000 (100,000 x (£10 - £2.50)), upon which he pays CGT.

## (b) Exercise price set below market value
If the option exercise price per share is set below market value at the date of the option grant:
- *no tax will be due on the grant of the option;*
- *income tax (and potentially also national insurance) will be due on the exercise of the option, on the original discount (i.e. the amount by which the market value exceeded the exercise price);*
- *capital gains tax will be due on the eventual sale of the shares on growth in value from the date of the option grant.*

**Alston Intelligence Limited: EMI options granted with an exercise price below market value**

*Grant of options*

As with the previous example, the market value of an ordinary share in Alston Intelligence is £3 (before restrictions), and £2.50 after restrictions.

Options are granted to Elizabeth Hartside over 10,000 shares, but this time with an exercise price of 10p per share. Elizabeth is treated more generously because she has been with the company for 15 years and it is felt fair to discount her option exercise price to give her some inbuilt reward in recognition of the contribution she has already made to the company.

*Exercise of the options*

Three years later, Elizabeth exercises her options. She pays 10p per share. At this point, she becomes liable for income tax on her original discount. Income tax is due on £24,000 (10,000 x (£2.50 - £0.10)).

*Sale of the shares*

After a further five years, she sells her shares for £10 each. She has made a total further gain of £75,000 (10,000 x (£10 - £2.50)), upon which she pays CGT.

## (c) Disqualifying event

Things may get more complicated if there is an EMI *disqualifying event*.

### (i) *What is an EMI disqualifying event?*

Each of the following is a disqualifying event under an EMI option:

The company whose shares are under option becomes controlled by another company (this does not include where the controlling company is a corporate trustee of an employee ownership trust).

The company ceasing to meet the trading activities requirements.

The optionholder ceasing to be an employee, or ceasing to meet the working time requirements.

Changes are made to the terms of an existing EMI option which:
- *increases the market value of the shares under option; or*
- *means that the option would no longer meet the requirements of the EMI legislation.*

Changes are made to the share capital of the company whose shares are under option that affect the value of the shares under option, where the rights of any shares in the company (not just the shares under option) are changed or a restriction is imposed or lifted, and where the alteration either:

- *means that the option would no longer meet the requirements of the EMI legislation; or*
- *is done for non-commercial reasons, or has as a main purpose the increase in the market value of those shares.*

There is any conversion of the shares under option into shares of a different class, unless the conversion is of one original class of shares into one new class of shares, all shares of the original class are converted, and immediately before the conversion either:

- *most of the shares of the original class are held otherwise than by or for the benefit of directors or employees of the company, an associated company of the company, directors or employees of an associated company; or*
- *the company is employee-controlled as a result of holdings of shares of the original class.*

A CSOP option is granted that causes the EMI individual limit to be breached for a particular employee.

If the company was eligible to grant an EMI option on the grounds that it was preparing to carry on a qualifying trade, either those preparations cease or the period of two years after the grant date expires without the trade commencing.

### (ii) What happens if there is a disqualifying event?
If a disqualifying event happens, then unless existing EMI options are exercised within 90 days, how they are taxed will change.

Instead of any growth in share value from the date of option grant being subject to CGT:

- *growth in value up to the date of the disqualifying event will continue to be subject to CGT, but*
- *any further growth, up to the date of option exercise, will be subject to income tax (and possibly also National Insurance).*

If the optionholder retains the shares after option exercise and they grow further in value, the tax on that further growth will revert to income tax.

### Alston Intelligence Limited: impact on EMI options of a disqualifying event

#### *Grant of options*
Mo Stanhope has been granted EMI options over 10,000 shares with an exercise price of £2.50 per share.

#### *Disqualifying event*
Mo resigns from the company after three years.

The terms of his option allow him to exercise 6,000 of his options but the other 4,000 lapse. On the date he leaves, each share has a value of £5. He exercises the 6,000 options a year after leaving, when each share has a value of £7.

On exercise, he is liable for income tax on £2 per share (£7 - £5).

He holds on to the shares for a further two years and then sells each share for £10. Capital gains tax is due on (i) the growth in value per share from £2.50 to £5 and (ii) the further growth in value from £7 to £10.

If instead Mo had exercised his options within 90 days of leaving, he would not have incurred an income tax liability. The only tax he would have paid would have been CGT on his eventual sale, on the difference between his £2.50 exercise price and his £10 sale price.

## 12.10   Corporation tax
The employing company will be able to claim relief against corporation tax in respect of option gains, subject to meeting the conditions (see Chapter 19).

## 12.11   Key steps in granting EMI options
A company planning to grant EMI options should consider the following:

### (a) Eligibility
Do the company and its shares meet the eligibility requirements and are the intended optionholders full-time employees?

## (b) What should the terms of the option be?

When will the optionholder be allowed to exercise the option (for example, the option could be exercised after a specified period of time or the number of shares over which it can be exercised could increase over time – this process is called *vesting*)?

Should the right to exercise the option be conditional on a performance target having been achieved? Any target should be measurable (*"you can exercise your option if we think you've done a good job"* leaves too much discretion with the company – the optionholder will not know what they have to do to be able to exercise it).

What happens if the optionholder leaves before exercising their option? Do all the options lapse or does it depend on how long the optionholder has been with the company, why they left, or does it take both these factors into account?

What should the option exercise price be – market value, below market value or above market value?

## (c) What is the market value of a share?

It is not a requirement to agree the market value of shares in a company at the time of granting EMI options with HM Revenue and Customs but it is generally recommended.

The key tax benefit of EMI options is that growth in value from market value at the date of option grant is lowly taxed (CGT rather than income tax). So when the option is exercised, it is therefore important to know what the market value of a share was at the grant date, because if the option exercise price was set at a level less than market value income tax will be due on the difference.

It is more straightforward to determine this at the time of grant rather than years later when the option is exercised, and it is possible to ask HM Revenue and Customs to agree a market value figure.

## (d) EMI option agreement

The terms of an EMI option must be recorded in a written agreement between the employee and the grantor of the option (this will generally be the company but it could be an existing shareholder).

An EMI option agreement must:

- *state the date when the option is granted;*
- *state the number of shares over which the option is granted and the exercise price per share;*
- *state that the option is granted under ITEPA 2003 Schedule 5 – in other words that it is an EMI option;*
- *set out when and how the option may be exercised;*
- *set out any performance conditions;*
- *State any risk of the shares being forfeited;*
- *be capable of being exercised within ten years (but the agreement can (i) still have a performance condition which if not met within ten years would prevent the option being exercised, and (ii) still link the right to exercise to a certain event happening, so if it did not happen within ten years the option could not be exercised);*
- *prohibit the optionholder from transferring the option to any other person (although transfer to the personal representatives of a deceased shareholder is permitted);*
- *prohibit option exercise more than twelve months after the optionholder's death;*
- *contain details of any restrictions affecting the shares subject to the option. As a minimum, it is recommended that the option agreement refers to specific clauses containing restrictions in the company's articles of association and (if there is one) its shareholder agreement (restrictions are most likely to be found in these documents) and make a copy of them available to the optionholder; and*
- *contain a statement by the optionholder that they meet the working time requirement, a copy of which must be provided to the optionholder within seven days. Alternatively, this declaration can be made in a separate document.*

The optionholder must be supplied with a copy of the option within seven days of its signature.

### (e)  Communication
If employees holding EMI options do not understand how they work, all or most of their incentive value will be lost. It is therefore

strongly recommended, as a minimum, to prepare a plain English guide for optionholders, perhaps as a Q&A. Some companies go further and arrange a presentation or meeting for optionholders, providing an opportunity for them to ask questions. This is especially worth considering where options are being granted to a small number of key people.

### (f) Internal approval
Where (as will normally be the case) EMI options are being granted by a company over new issue shares, the company's directors will need to approve the grant.

Depending on the company's articles of association and any shareholders' agreement, shareholder approval may also be required.

### (g) HMRC registration
Where EMI options are being granted over a company's shares for the first time, the company must notify HM Revenue and Customs online that it has established an EMI option plan, after which it must then give notification of the grant of each option. All of this must be completed within 92 days of the option grant.

Any subsequent option grants must also be notified to HM Revenue and Customs within 92 days of the date of grant of that option.

### (h) Annual return
Where EMI options have been granted over a company's shares, the company must complete an HM Revenue and Customs online annual return each year. This must be done following the end of each tax year, by 6 July.

### To recap:
- Any company wishing to reward key employees through share options should consider whether EMI options are available.
- Not all companies are eligible for EMI options and it is important to check the conditions, of which the main ones relate to:
  - *maximum size of company*
  - *independence of the company*
  - *nature of the company's trade*

- *the* company having a permanent establishment in the UK
- *the* hours worked by the employee.
- EMI options may be offered to selected employees and there is no same terms requirement.
- If a company that is controlled by an employee ownership trust wishes to grant EMI options, this must be over new issue shares (or shares held by other shareholders) and not shares in the EOT.
- There is no obligation to exercise the option at the end of the option period
- For any private company granting EMI options, market value does not have to be agreed in advance with HMRC but it is generally recommended to do so.
- Option gains are not subject to income tax or National Insurance. Instead, CGT is charged when the shares are eventually sold.
- A company's EMI scheme must be registered with HMRC within 92 days of the first option grant. Each grant must be notified to HMRC within the same period and an annual return completed each year.

# 13 CSOP options

## 13.1 Introduction

Chapter 5 included an overview of CSOP options as a way to involve selected employees in a company's ownership. This chapter provides further detail and will assist a company which is contemplating using CSOP options as a way for its key employees to become shareholders, to:

- *evaluate whether it is the right approach;*
- *confirm whether it is eligible to grant CSOP options; and*
- *understand the main steps in creating and then operating a CSOP option scheme.*

## 13.2 When CSOP options may be suitable

As has been mentioned in Chapter 2, a company which has become majority employee-owned may wish to introduce a separate share ownership arrangement for its key people. It will not be possible to do this under a SIP or SAYE option scheme, as each of these must involve all employees on the same or similar terms.

The company should generally start by considering EMI options, but not every company will be eligible. For example, it may not operate the right kind of trade or it may be too large (with gross assets of £30 million or more or more than 250 full-time equivalent employees).

There are fewer eligibility requirements for CSOP options than there are for EMI, so they are worth considering when EMI is not available.

## 13.3 How do CSOP options work?

As with EMI options, a chosen participant is granted an option to acquire a specified number of shares in their employer company (or its holding company) at a fixed exercise price. However, a key difference is that the exercise price of a CSOP must not be less than market value at the date of grant.

Key tax benefit of CSOP options are:

- *no income tax or National Insurance is payable when the option is exercised; and*

- *tax only becomes due when, following the exercise of the option, the shares are eventually sold, at which point the tax due will be CGT.*

For CSOP option gains to be income tax free, options must normally be capable of exercise only between three and ten years following the grant. However, in certain circumstances they can be exercised within the first three years without adverse tax consequences. See 13.9.

## 13.4    What are the financial limits?
CSOP options may not be granted to a single individual over shares with a market value (measured at the date of grant) of more than £30,000.

Unlike with EMI options, a company over which CSOP options have been granted is not subject to any aggregate limit on the value of options.

## 13.5    Is your company eligible to grant CSOP options?
Where CSOP options are to be granted over shares in a private company, it must not be controlled by another company. The company can however be controlled by an employee ownership trust with a corporate trustee.

The definition of *control* is the same as for EMI options: see Chapter 12.

## 13.6    Which employees can be granted CSOP options?
A CSOP option may only be granted to an employee if the following requirements are met:
- *they must be an employee or director of the company whose shares are subject to the options, or of a subsidiary;*
- *if a director, they must be full-time (but there is no such requirement for non-director employees); and*
- *they must not already hold 30% of the company's shares (including any shares held by their business partner, spouse, civil partner, parents, children, other relatives in the direct line and certain trusts).*

## 13.7 What kinds of share can CSOP options be granted over?

CSOP options must be granted over ordinary shares which are fully paid up and not redeemable. It is possible to grant options over a separate class of ordinary shares in certain circumstances.

### (a) Ordinary shares

Ordinary share capital means all the issued share capital (by whatever name called) of the company, other than capital which carries a right to a fixed rate dividend and no other right to share in the profits of the company.

HM Revenue and Customs will treat as ordinary share capital shares which have no rights to receive dividends and shares which have a right to the greater of a specified sum or the dividend paid in respect of another class of share.

### (b) Fully paid up

Fully paid up means that the subscription price for the shares is paid before the shares are issued. Shares issued without full payment of at least their nominal value will not be fully paid.

If CSOP options are to be granted over shares that are already issued (i.e. already held by an existing shareholder), it will be necessary to check that at least the nominal value of those shares has been paid up at the time of option grant.

If CSOP options are to be granted over newly issued shares (that is, new shares will be issued when the option is exercised), the option exercise price must be at least nominal value and must be paid on exercise.

### (c) Not redeemable

A share is redeemable if it is to be redeemed by the company or liable to be redeemed at the option of the company or its holder.

### (d) Granting options over a separate class of ordinary share

Unlike with EMI options, a separate class of shares may only be used for grants of CSOP options if the shares of that class are regarded as either *open market shares* or *employee control shares*.

This requirement also applies to grants of SAYE options and is summarised in 11.4.

## 13.8 What are the main differences between EMI and CSOP options?

The following table summarises the key differences:

| | EMI | CSOP |
|---|---|---|
| Company | • Must be independent<br>• Must not have gross assets of £30 million or more or 250 or more full-time equivalent employees<br>• Must have a qualifying trade<br>• Must have a permanent UK establishment<br>• Subsidiaries must be qualifying subsidiaries | • Must be independent |
| Employees | • Company can choose who participates<br>• Full-time only<br>• Must not have a material interest<br>• Ceasing to be an employee (or full-time employee) is a disqualifying event | • Company can choose who participates<br>• Part-time employees or full-time directors<br>• Must not have a material interest<br>• Ceasing to be an employee or director does not affect the tax treatment |
| Shares | • Must be fully paid ordinary shares, not redeemable | • Must be fully paid ordinary shares, not redeemable<br>• Special rules apply if there is more than one class of share |
| Option exercise price | • May be set at any level (but this will impact on tax treatment) | • Must be at least market value at date of option grant |
| Tax treatment | • No income tax or NI on grant of option<br>• No income tax or NI on | • No income tax or NI on grant of option<br>• No income tax or NI on |

| | option exercise, unless exercise price is below market value at grant date<br>• CGT on eventual sale | option exercise<br>• CGT on eventual sale |
|---|---|---|
| Financial limit | • £250,000 per employee<br>• £3,000,000 overall | • £30,000 per employee |
| Minimum period between option grant and exercise | • None | • Normally three years |

## 13.9 Conditions for favourable tax treatment

### (a) Ceasing to be an employee

Although a three-year period must normally have passed if CSOP options are to be exercised without an income tax liability, this does not apply in the following circumstances:

- *the optionholder leaves due to injury, disability, redundancy or retirement and exercises their option within six months of leaving;*
- *the optionholder's employment is transferred to another employer under TUPE and they exercise within six months of the transfer;*
- *where the company employing the optionholder is a subsidiary of the company over whose shares the options are granted, the employer company is transferred outside the group and the optionholder exercises within six months of the transfer; or*
- *the optionholder's death.*

### (b) Change of control of the company over whose shares the option is granted

A CSOP option may also be exercised within three years without income tax if the company is taken over for cash and the takeover is structured as a general offer, a court-sanctioned scheme of arrangement, a non-UK reorganisation arrangement or under the compulsory "squeeze out" or "sell out" provisions of the Companies Act 2006 *(sections 979 and 983).*

There are strict requirements for timing of option exercises under this facility.

## 13.10   Corporation tax

The employing company will be able to claim relief against corporation tax in respect of option gains, subject to meeting the conditions (see Chapter 19).

## 13.11   Key steps in granting CSOP options

A company planning to grant CSOP options should consider the following:

### (a)  Eligibility

Do the company and its shares meet the eligibility requirements and is each intended optionholder an employee or a full-time director?

### (b)  What should the terms of the option be?

*(i)   When will the optionholder be allowed to exercise the option?*
The option might be allowed to be exercised after a specified period of time or the number of shares over which it can be exercised may increase over time – this process is called *vesting*). For a CSOP option, exercise will normally be after a minimum period of three years.

*(ii)   Should the right to exercise the option be conditional on a performance target having been achieved?*
Any target should be measurable, as for EMI options.

*(iii)   What happens if the optionholder leaves before exercising their option?*
Will all the options lapse or will it depend upon how long the optionholder has been with the company or why they left (or take both these factors into account)?  Should any right for leavers to exercise their options (or some of them) only apply if they leave in circumstances where there is no income tax charge on exercise within three years (see 13.9)?

*(iv)   What should the option exercise price be?*
For a CSOP option, the exercise price must be at least market value at the date when the option is granted.

### (c) What is the market value of a share?

The market value of shares in a private company must be agreed with HM Revenue and Customs at the time of granting CSOP options.

As with EMI options, the key tax benefit of CSOP options is that growth in value from market value at the date of option grant is lowly taxed (CGT rather than income tax). However, unlike with EMI options, the exercise price must not be less than market value at the date of grant – if it is less, the options will not have CSOP tax status.

In determining the market value of a share which is subject to restrictions, any resulting downwards impact on that share's value is to be disregarded when determining market value.

### (d) CSOP option plan rules

It is necessary to prepare a set of CSOP plan rules which comply with the statutory requirements, and the company must then certify that they do. Each grant of CSOP options will then be recorded in an option certificate personal to the optionholder which states that the option is granted under those rules.

### (e) Communication

If employees holding CSOP options do not understand how they work, all or most of their incentive value will be lost. As with EMI, it is therefore strongly recommended, as a minimum, to prepare a plain English guide for optionholders or even to arrange a presentation or meeting for optionholders, providing an opportunity for them to ask questions. This is especially worth considering where options are being granted to a small number of key people.

### (f) Internal approval

Where (as will normally be the case) CSOP options are being granted by a company over new issue shares, the company's directors will need to approve the grant.

Depending on the company's articles of association and any shareholders' agreement, shareholder approval may also be required.

### (g) HMRC registration

A new CSOP plan must be registered with HM Revenue and Customs online by 6 July following the end of the tax year in which the first CSOP options were granted or awards made.

### (h) Annual return

A company whose shares are the subject of CSOP options must then complete an HM Revenue and Customs online annual return each year. This must be done following the end of each tax year, by 6 July.

## 13.12  CSOP options – an example

**Brougham Transport Limited**

Brougham Transport develops and manufactures batteries for electric delivery vehicles. It isn't eligible to grant EMI options because it has 260 full-time employees.

It agrees with HM Revenue and Customs a market value (unrestricted) of an ordinary share at £2, and grants CSOP options to Emilia Dacre over 15,000 shares, using up the whole of her £30,000 CSOP personal limit. The options are exercisable if Emilia is still an employee after three years but early exercise is permitted if the company is sold within that period.

Two years later, the company's directors are contacted by Solway Propulsion Limited with an offer to purchase the company for £8 per share in cash.

The company has two shareholders (one of which is an employee ownership trust), which would increase to three if Emilia were to exercise her option and acquire shares. After careful consideration, the trustees decide that accepting the offer is in the best interests of beneficiaries, and the other shareholder also agrees to sell. The offer is therefore accepted, both existing shareholders enter into a share sale agreement with Solway Propulsion, Emilia exercises her option and under its terms then becomes bound to sell her shares.

Emilia has made a total gain of £90,000 (£120,000 sale price less £30,000 option exercise price). Because she has exercised her options before the three year anniversary of grant, she will be liable for income tax on her option gains (and also National Insurance, because she is able to convert her shares into cash) unless she can claim an exemption. None is available, though, because the sale has been structured as a sale agreement.

Had it instead been structured as a general offer to all shareholders, she would not have been liable for income tax or National Insurance, instead paying CGT on her option gains.

**To recap:**
- CSOP options may be suitable where EMI options are not available.
- CSOP options may be offered to selected employees and there is no same terms requirement.
- The conditions for eligibility to grant CSOP options are less stringent than for EMI options but the financial limits are significantly lower.
- They may only be granted to employees or full-time directors.
- If a company that is controlled by an employee ownership trust wishes to grant CSOP options, this must be over new issue shares (or shares held by other shareholders) and not shares in the EOT.
- There is no obligation to exercise the option at the end of the option period.
- For any private company granting CSOP options, market value must to be agreed in advance with HMRC.
- Option gains are not subject to income tax or National Insurance. Instead, CGT is charged when the shares are eventually sold.
- Registration with HMRC is required

# 14  Other ways for employees to acquire shares

## 14.1  Why it may sometimes be necessary to consider other ways for employees to acquire shares

As discussed above, many employee-owned companies will not wish to have any form of personal share ownership, preferring all the shares to be held permanently in an employee trust, but as acknowledged in previous chapters, this will not always be the case.

Some may want a proportion of shares to be available for personal ownership by *all their employees*, and are likely to consider structuring this through a SIP or SAYE options if they wish to take advantage of statutory tax breaks.

Alternatively, or additionally, other companies may wish to involve their *key employees* in share ownership, with EMI or CSOP options potentially available to reduce the tax payable on option gains.

But there may be circumstances where none of these offer the right solution. This chapter looks at the main alternatives.

## 14.2  Non-approved options

Options which are not granted under any of the statutory tax approved option plans (EMI and CSOP for selected employees, SAYE for all employees) are known as non-approved or unapproved options.

This does not mean that they somehow break tax rules or otherwise do not comply with the law. It simply signifies that they do not confer tax advantages, so participants will pay income tax, and sometimes also National Insurance, on any option gains.

### (a)  How are non-approved options taxed?

Options granted by reason of employment are treated for tax purposes as employment-related securities options. The key term in the legislation is *"by reason of employment"*. This term includes an individual who is a director but not an employee and can also include a situation where options are granted over shares of a company that does not employ the optionholder (or of which the optionholder is not a director).

Options granted to an individual who is genuinely self-employed and not an employee or director will not be treated as employment-related securities options. This will result in a different tax treatment to that covered in earlier in this chapter (see 14.2(e) for further information).

When a non-approved option is exercised, the optionholder must pay income tax on the difference between the price they pay and the value of the shares at the time of exercise (the *option gain*).

Depending on the circumstances, National Insurance may also be due. Where National Insurance is due, this will be both employee's (primary) and employer's (secondary) National Insurance.

It is possible to include as a term of the option that the optionholder will pay the employer's National Insurance, as well as employee's National Insurance and income tax. In that case, the amount of the option gain on which income tax is due will be calculated after employer's National Insurance.

If a non-approved option is exercised by the personal representatives of an optionholder who has died, no income tax or National Insurance liability will arise.

### Non-approved options: when is National Insurance due on option gains, in addition to income tax?

National Insurance will be due if the shares acquired on option exercise are *readily convertible assets*.

In summary, shares will be readily convertible assets if any of the following apply:
- *there are trading arrangements for those shares (this would always be the case for listed company shares, and may also be the case in a private company which had set up an internal market for its shares)*
- *they are not ordinary shares*
- *they are not fully paid up*
- *they are redeemable*
- *they are shares in a company controlled by another company (unless the controlling company is listed) or*
- *they are shares in a company which is not (broadly) in the same group as the company employing the optionholder.*

## (b) When is the tax on option gains payable?

This will depend on whether the shares are readily convertible assets.

If they are readily convertible assets, income tax and National Insurance must be paid under PAYE. As this means the company employing the optionholder is responsible for ensuring these taxes are paid to HM Revenue and Customs, it will be important that it has the right under the option plan to recover them from the optionholder.

If they are not readily convertible assets, income tax is paid by the optionholder under self-assessment.

## (c) What tax will be payable if the shares are restricted securities?

If the shares acquired on option exercise are *restricted securities*, the tax treatment of option exercise is more nuanced. The rules are complex and a detailed analysis is beyond the scope of this book, but a summary of how restricted securities (which includes shares subject to restrictions) are taxed is set out in 14.5, and an example of the impact of awarding options over restricted securities is set out below.

### Exercise of a non-approved option over restricted shares
### A worked example

Richard Dufton has an option to acquire 1,000 new shares in his employer, Flakebridge Associates Limited, a marketing and design agency, at 50 pence per share. If he were to leave following option exercise for a specified "bad leaver" reason, the shares would have to be offered for sale at the lower of their then market value and the price paid for them when he exercised his option. The value of the shares (after taking into account this restriction) when he exercises his option is 80 pence per share; the full (unrestricted) value is £1 per share. Richard later sells the shares for £2 each.

### *No election made*

If no election is made on exercise of his option, Richard will be charged to income tax (and possibly National Insurance) on the acquisition, on the difference between 50 pence and 80 pence per share (as well as paying the 50 pence per share exercise price).

When he eventually sells the shares, he is liable to pay income tax (and possibly National Insurance) on 40p per share (20% of the sale price, because on exercising his option he paid the exercise price and income tax together representing 80% of the full value), that is in total £2 x 20% x 1,000 = £400.

Capital gains tax (ignoring the annual exempt amount) is due on £800, that is the total sale price of £2,000 less:

£500 (the amount he paid for his shares)

£300 (the amount on which he was taxed on exercise of his option), and

£400 (the amount of income tax/NI on selling the shares).

### An election is made
If instead Richard makes a restricted securities election when he exercises his option, he will pay income tax/National Insurance at that time on the difference between 50 pence and £1 per share.

On his sale of the shares, there will be no further income tax/National Insurance to pay. He will pay capital gains on £1 per share, that is on the growth from £1 to £2.

## (d) Is any further tax due?
When the optionholder disposes of their shares, CGT will be due on any growth in the shares' value between the date of option exercise and the date of disposal.

## (e) What is the position where options are granted to self-employed individuals?
Some companies grant non-approved options to individuals who are not employees or directors, for example consultants providing particular services or advice.

Here the tax treatment will be different, unless the optionholder is shown to be an employee or director who is receiving options over shares in any company in that capacity.

In short, the value of an option granted to a self-employed individual will be treated as income. This will require the option itself to be valued, and that value will be different from the value of the underlying shares.

Exercise of the option will not give rise to a tax charge.

If the option is exercised and the resulting shares are eventually disposed of, the individual will pay CGT on their gain.

### (f) Who is eligible to be granted non-approved options?

A company can grant non-approved options to selected employees or directors, or to advisers.

### (g) Are there any financial limits on non-approved options

There are no limitations under tax legislation on the value of options that may be granted to a single individual or overall by a company.

However, as with any other arrangement involving personal share ownership, the company will wish to place its own overall limit on how many options may be granted, to limit dilution of other shareholders.

### (h) Corporation tax

As with other forms of employee share option, the employing company will be able to claim relief against corporation tax in respect of option gains, subject to meeting the conditions (see Chapter 19).

### (i) Key steps in granting non-approved options

A company planning to grant non-approved options should consider the following:

### (i) *What should the terms of the option be?*

When will the optionholder be allowed to exercise the option (for example, the option can be exercised after a specified period of time or the number of shares over which it can be exercised can increase over time (*vesting*).

Should the right to exercise the option be conditional on a performance target having been achieved? Targets must be measurable.

What happens if the optionholder leaves before exercising their option? Do all the options lapse or does it depend on how long the optionholder has been with the company, why they left (or take both these factors into account)?

What should the option exercise price be – market value, less than market value or above market value?

## (ii) Option plan rules

It is necessary to prepare a set of option plan rules. Each grant of options will then be recorded in an option certificate personal to the optionholder, which will state that the option is granted under those rules. Alternatively, options can be granted under an option agreement between the company and the optionholder.

## (iii) Communication

As with any option scheme, if employees holding options do not understand how they work, all or most of their incentive value will be lost. It is therefore recommended that an explanation be provided to the optionholder, either in the form of a written guide or by way of a presentation.

## (iv) Internal approval

Where (as will normally be the case) non-approved options are being granted by a company over new issue shares, the company's directors will need to approve the grant.

Depending on the company's articles of association and any shareholders' agreement, shareholder approval may also be required.

## (v) HMRC registration

A new non-approved plan must be registered with HM Revenue and Customs online by 6 July following the end of the tax year in which it was established.

Although HM Revenue and Customs has published guidance stating that a company only has to register a non-approved option if a reportable event occurs during the tax year, in practice the non-approved plan will have to have been registered by the end of the tax year if options have been granted, because the option grant will be a reportable event.

## (vi) Annual return

A company whose shares are the subject of non-approved options must complete an HM Revenue and Customs annual return each year online. This must be done following the end of each tax year, by 6 July.

### Non-approved options case study: Swindale Manufacturing Limited

Swindale Manufacturing, which designs and manufactures bespoke computer systems, is currently wholly owned by an employee ownership trust which has a corporate trustee. Swindale wishes to grant share options to each of its three executive directors, over a special class of shares which do not have voting rights. It is too large to grant EMI options, having 300 full-time employees, and it is not permitted to grant CSOP options because the non-voting shares will be ineligible.

The company therefore decides to grant non-approved options, each optionholder being granted an option to acquire 20,000 shares. The options are granted by the company, so if exercised it will issue new shares. They are exercisable after a three year period if the optionholder is then still an employee. The option exercise price is set at £1 per share which is considered to be equal to market value. Because the options are non-approved, there is no facility to agree market value at the date of option grant with HM Revenue and Customs, and no need to do so because tax due on exercise will simply be based on the difference between the exercise price and value at the date of exercise.

After three years, each share is now worth £5 (value after taking restrictions into account). One optionholder, Anita Skelton, decides to exercise her options in full, paying £20,000. As her shares are now worth £100,000 in total, she is liable for income tax on her £80,000 option gain. She may also be liable for employee's (primary) National Insurance because the employee ownership trust has a corporate trustee (so Swindale may be treated as controlled by another company, making the shares readily convertible assets), and Swindale itself would then be liable for employer's (secondary) National Insurance. If the shares are considered to be readily convertible assets, income tax and National Insurance must be paid under PAYE.

If the shares are restricted, so their value on exercise is greater than £5 per share, Anita will pay further income tax/National Insurance on sale (or when the restrictions are lifted), unless she signs an election (in which her tax liability on exercise will be greater).

Here are two possible variations to this example:

*Variation 1:* *If the employee ownership had individual trustees rather than a corporate trustee, there would be no National Insurance on Anita's option gains unless arrangements were in place enabling her to sell her shares. Anita would instead pay income tax under self-assessment.*

*Variation 2:* *The terms of Anita's options required her to be responsible for the employer's National Insurance. If the shares are readily convertible assets, she will pay both employee's and employer's National Insurance on her option gains plus income tax on her option gains net of employer's National Insurance.*

## 14.3  Purchase of ordinary shares

A company wishing to involve a relatively small number of its key employees or directors in personal share ownership in a way which involves them making a personal financial commitment could consider inviting them to purchase ordinary shares.

### (a)  Tax treatment

There is no income tax/National Insurance charge if the price paid on acquisition is at least market value.  If the price is below market value, a tax charge will arise.

Any such tax will be payable either under self-assessment or PAYE, depending on whether the shares are readily convertible assets. See 14.2.

### (b)  Who is eligible to acquire ordinary shares?

A company can invite any individual to acquire ordinary shares.

### (c)  Are there any financial limits on the purchase of ordinary shares?

There are no limitations under tax legislation on the value of ordinary shares that may be acquired by a single individual or overall within a company.

However, as with any other arrangement involving personal share ownership, the company will wish to place its own overall cap on the number of shares which may be issued, to limit the dilution of other shareholders (and if the company is majority owned by an employee ownership trust, to ensure that its holding remains above 50%).

### (d) Corporation tax

A corporation tax deduction cannot be claimed in connection with purchases of ordinary shares (unlike with share options and awards of free shares under a SIP).

### (e) Key steps in issuing ordinary shares

A company planning to issue ordinary shares should consider the following:

#### (i) What is the company's current value?

It is advisable to take professional advice from an experienced company valuation expert. If the purchase price of the shares is less than their market value, there will be a tax charge on the individual who acquires them.

#### (ii) On what terms should the shares be held?

What happens if the shareholder leaves? Are they required to offer their shares for sale, and if so, at what price? Does the price depend on their reason for leaving?

Should other provisions be added to the articles of association at the same time, for example "drag along" and "tag along" under which if the majority shareholder ever wishes to sell to a third party it can require other shareholders also to do so (and entitle them to be bought out).

#### (iii) Amend articles of association

It may be necessary to change the company's articles of association, although this may not always be the case. This will require shareholder approval.

#### (iv) Subscription agreement

Each employee acquiring ordinary shares should sign a share subscription agreement with the company, and pay the prescribed purchase price for their shares.

#### (v) Communication

As with options and other forms of employee share ownership, it is strongly recommended, as a minimum, to prepare a plain English guide for employees acquiring ordinary shares, perhaps as a Q&A. Some companies will arrange a presentation or meeting for participating employees, providing an opportunity for them to ask questions. This is especially worth considering where ordinary shares are being offered to a small number of key people.

## (vi) Internal approval

The company's directors will need to approve the issue of the shares. A shareholder resolution will be required to approve any changes to the company's articles of association.

## (vii) HMRC registration

A company which issues ordinary shares must register this with HM Revenue and Customs online by 6 July following the end of the tax year in which the shares were first issued.

## (viii) Companies House

Notification will need to be given to Companies House of the issue of any new shares.

## (ix) Annual return

A company which has issued ordinary shares to employees or directors must then complete an HM Revenue and Customs annual return online each year. This must be done following the end of each tax year, by 6 July.

## (f) In summary

In practice, it is often difficult for employees, even those at a senior level, to fund the purchase of shares, other than for small amounts at a low purchase price. It is also often challenging to find a willing third party lender, and even where funds are available many senior employees often may not wish to make significant levels of personal investment. For all these reasons, it is not likely to be common for employees to purchase ordinary shares in significant amounts.

**Example - Towcett Restaurants Limited – directors purchase ordinary shares**

Towcett Restaurants has recently become 100% owned by an employee ownership trust, which holds 10,000 ordinary shares. It wishes to establish a share ownership arrangement under which its three executive directors (Rory, Kobi and Eliza) will each be invited to purchase ordinary shares, paying a price equal to market value. It believes that these directors will have a strong incentive to perform if they have invested their own money.

The company is able to create a borrowing facility with its bank, under which each director is able to borrow funds equal to the purchase price. The intention is that the company will pay dividends, which the directors can use to fund the repayment of bank loans and interest payments.

Each director accepts their invitation. The company issues 589 new ordinary shares to each director, 1,767 in total, bringing the total issued shares to 11,767, held as follows:
Employee ownership trust – 10,000 (85%)
Rory – 589 (5%)
Kobi – 589 (5%)
Eliza - 589 (5%)

## 14.4  Nil or partly paid shares

This involves employees or directors being invited to purchase shares in their company, in a similar way to that discussed in 14.3. Where it differs, however, is that the shares do not have to be paid for immediately. The buyer's obligation to pay is deferred until a later date, and such payment made be made in a single payment or in instalments.

### (a)  Tax treatment

There is no income tax/National Insurance charge on the acquisition of the shares if the price to be paid is at least market value when the shares are acquired.  If the price is below market value, an income tax charge will arise, payable either under self-assessment or PAYE, depending on whether the shares are readily convertible assets. See 14.2.

There will, however, generally be an annual income tax charge on notional interest on the unpaid amount. This works as follows:

- *if interest is charged on the unpaid amount at a rate at least equal to the HM Revenue and Customs official rate, there will be no tax charge*
- *if no interest is charged, income tax is due annually on the amount of interest that would have been paid at the official rate*
- *if interest is charged at below the official rate, income tax is due annually on the difference.*

Income tax is not due, however, where:

- *the employee's loans are no more than £10,000*
- *the employee has died*
- *more than seven years have passed since employment ceased*
- *the employee would have been granted income tax relief on interest on any third party loan to buy the shares*
- *if the shares are of a particular class, all of the shares in that class are acquired for no payment or for a payment less than the market value and either:*
  - *the majority of the shares of the class are not employment-related securities or*
  - *the company is "employee-controlled" through the shares of that class*

*"Employee-controlled"* has a specific statutory definition. Under ITEPA 2003, section 421H a company is employee-controlled by virtue of shares of a particular class if:

- *the majority of the shares of that class (excluding any held by or for an associated company) are held by or for the benefit of the company's employees (or employees of a company it controls) and*
- *those employees are able, as holders of those shares, to control the company.*

### Hesket Services Limited – directors acquire shares and pay later

Hesket Services manufactures a range of agricultural products. It is 100% owned by an employee ownership trust (which holds 1,000 shares). However, the trustees have approved an arrangement under which two of the company's executive directors will be invited to subscribe for 56 new shares each, increasing the number of issued shares to 1,112 and resulting in the trust holding 90% and the two directors holding 5% each.

Each share has a value of £500 so the total purchase price for each director is £28,000.

The company agrees that they can each pay in instalments, paying £5,600 per year over the next five years.

It is also agreed that should either of them leave, they must (a) offer their shares for sale and (b) pay the balance of the purchase price. They are also informed that if the company were to become insolvent, they should expect to be required to pay the balance of the purchase price, because a liquidator will treat it as a debt due to the company

## (b) Eligibility

A company can invite any individual to acquire ordinary shares in this way. However, any employee (or other individual) who agrees to do so is taking on an inescapable liability to pay (unless the company waives its right to payment in future, in which case an income tax charge will be due on the amount waived). That liability will remain in place even if the company's shares subsequently fall in value or if the company becomes insolvent.

## (c) Are there any financial limits on the purchase of nil or partly paid ordinary shares?

There are none.

## (d) Corporation tax

See Chapter 19.

## (e) Key steps in issuing nil or partly paid ordinary shares

A company planning to issue shares which are nil or partly paid shares should consider the following:

### (i) What is the current value?

As with the purchase of fully paid shares, it is advisable to take professional advice from an experienced company valuation expert. If the purchase price of the shares is less than their market value, there will be a tax charge on the individual who acquires them.

### (ii) On what terms should the shares be held?

When should payments be made and in what circumstances should the full amount of any outstanding sum be required to be paid (for example, if the shareholder leaves)?

Are they required to offer their shares for sale, and if so, at what price? Does the price depend on why they are leaving?

Should other provisions be added to the articles of association at the same time, for example "drag along" and "tag along" under which if the majority shareholder ever wishes to sell to a third party it can require other shareholders also to do so (and entitle them to be bought out)?

### (iii) Amend articles of association

It may be necessary to change the company's articles of association, although this may not always be the case. This will require shareholder approval.

### (iv) Subscription agreement

Each employee acquiring ordinary shares should sign a share subscription agreement with the company, and pay the prescribed purchase price (if any) for their shares.

### (v) Communication

As with options and other forms of employee share ownership, it is strongly recommended that the scheme be fully explained to the participants, either by issuing a written guide or through a presentation.

It is essential that it is made crystal clear to any individual invited to acquire nil or partly paid shares that they will ultimately be required to pay for them.

### (vi) Internal approval

The company's directors will need to approve the issue of the shares. A shareholder resolution will be required to approve changes to the company's articles of association.

### (vii) HMRC registration

The issue of nil paid shares must be registered with HM Revenue and Customs online by 6 July following the end of the tax year in which the shares were first issued.

### (viii) Companies House

Notification will need to be given to Companies House of any issue of new shares.

### (ix) Annual return

A company which has issued nil or partly paid ordinary shares to employees or directors must then complete an HM Revenue and Customs online annual return each year. This must be done following the end of each tax year, by 6 July.

## (f)  In summary

Nil or partly paid shares are not for the faint-hearted. Unlike options, which will only be exercised by the participator if the share value is higher than the exercise price, so they will have no immediate risk, nil or partly paid shares involve a commitment to pay the purchase price, albeit deferred. There have been situations where employees of companies have been issued shares on a nil paid basis, not understanding that they have also been taking on a liability to pay for them after a period of time, and when called on to pay, they find that the shares' value has fallen considerably. This has placed the affected employees in a most unattractive position and can cause distress and financial problems.

It is recommended that wherever possible nil or partly paid share arrangements be structured in a way that keeps liability to pay at a modest level (so that if an individual is called on to pay for the shares in any circumstances, that should not lead to their personal insolvency), and that where this is not possible these arrangements are made available only to individuals who fully understand and are willing to accept the risk. In any case, the risks for participants should always be fully explained.

## 14.5  Restricted securities

Shares can be subject to restrictions which adversely affect their value, such as restrictions on their transferability or a requirement to sell them for a reduced value if the person holding them ceases to be an employee.

The restricted securities legislation closed a tax loophole under which it was possible to create a class of share with a low value due to its having various restrictions attached to it. Shares of that class could therefore be transferred to employees at low cost. Over time, the restrictions would be lifted, increasing the shares' value, but not resulting in a tax charge until they were eventually sold, at which point the employee who had sold would be subject to CGT on the resulting growth in value.

### (a)  The tax treatment

The effect of the restricted securities legislation is to make any growth in a share's value which results from the lifting of restrictions subject to income tax (and potentially also National Insurance).

This tax charge will be additional to any which arises when the shares are first acquired, on their value at that time.[21]

Where an employee acquires shares which are subject to restrictions and these reduce the shares' value, the optionholder and the employer company can by agreement choose to sign a *restricted securities election* (also known as a *Section 431 election*). The effect of this is that:

- *the market value of the shares, for the purpose of determining whether there is a tax liability on acquisition, disregards any reduction caused by the restrictions, and so*
- *any future growth in value following acquisition by the employee is subject only to CGT.*

If no election is signed:

- *any income tax due on acquisition will be based on the reduced value per share caused by the restrictions, but*
- *a proportion of any subsequent growth in value will be subject to income tax (and possibly National Insurance), the rest being subject to CGT.*

Any restricted securities election must be signed by the employee and the company within fourteen days of the shares having been acquired, using a form approved by HM Revenue and Customs.

---

[21] There is generally no income tax liability on acquisition, where shares acquired directly (rather than through exercise of an option) are subject to forfeiture restrictions which do not last more than five years. This can enable an award of free shares to be made without triggering an immediate tax liability. However, when restrictions are lifted or fall away, tax will then become due on the full value of those shares at that time. A Section 431 election can be signed, as with any other kind of restricted shares or securities, for an immediate tax charge on the shares' unrestricted value. Alternatively, a Section 425 election can be signed, the effect of which will be a tax charge on their restricted value. In the latter case, further income tax will be due when the restrictions are lifted or fall away.

## (b) Other issues

Apart from tax treatment and the question of the Section 431 election, the issues associated with issuing restricted securities are similar to those covered in 14.3.

### Acquiring restricted shares - A worked example

John Colby purchases 2,000 new shares in his employer, Flakebridge Associates Limited, a manufacturer of specialist building products. If he were to leave following option exercise for a specified "bad leaver" reason, the shares must be offered for sale at the lower of their then market value and the price paid for them when he exercised his option. The value of the shares (after taking into account this restriction) when he acquires the shares is 80 pence per share; their full (unrestricted) value is £1 per share. John pays a purchase price of 80 pence per share.

John later sells the shares for £2 each.

#### No election made
If no election is made, John will be charged tax as follows – when he sells the shares:
- *Income tax (and possibly National Insurance) on 20% of the £2 sale price*
- *CGT on the £2 sale price less his 80 pence purchase price less the amount chargeable to income tax*

#### An election is made
If instead John makes a restricted securities election within fourteen days of acquiring the shares, he will pay:
- *income tax/National Insurance at that time on the difference between 80 pence and £1 per share.*
- *On his sale of the shares, there will be no further income tax/National Insurance to pay. He will pay capital gains on £1 per share, that is on the growth from £1 to £2.*

Because share value has risen significantly, he is ultimately in a better financial position by making the election, because more of the tax he pays is CGT rather than income tax and so at a lower rate. Had share value fallen (or risen by only a small amount), he would have been better off not making an election.

## 14.6  Growth shares

A company wishing to involve a relatively small number of its key employees or directors in personal share ownership could consider creating *growth shares,* as an alternative to EMI or CSOP options if these are not available (or their limits have been exceeded) and non-approved options.

Their potential attraction is that they enable participating employees to acquire shares with minimal immediate financial commitment and then to pay CGT, rather than income tax/National Insurance, on any subsequent growth in value.

How this works is that the company creates a new class of shares which will only entitle their holders to a stake in the company's value to the extent that it exceeds a certain level. This may be best illustrated with an example.

### Salkeld Construction Limited – growth shares

Salkeld Construction has a value of £5 million (this is based on an independent valuation). Currently wholly-owned by an employee ownership trust (which holds 100 ordinary shares), it wishes to put in place a growth share arrangement under which Meg Lazonby may acquire shares which entitle her to 5% of any growth in value of the company above £5.5 million.

This is done by changing the articles of association to say that if the company is ever sold or liquidated:

- under its existing ordinary shares, the trust will receive the first £5.5 million
- under the new growth shares, any excess above £5.5 million will be shared between Meg (through her holding of growth shares) as to 5% and the trust (through its holding of ordinary shares) as to 95%.

So if the company were sold for £10 million, the trust would receive £9,775,000 and Meg £225,000.

The company issues the new growth shares, 95 to the trust and 5 to Meg. Each share gives its holder an entitlement to 1% of any value above £5.5 million.

The person who has valued the company at £5 million also advises that, since the company's value must grow to £5.5 million before the growth shares acquire any value, their current value is very low, and they attribute a value of £5,000 to them.

Meg can therefore acquire her growth shares by either paying £5,000 or by paying a nominal amount and accepting an income tax/National Insurance charge on the difference between that and £5,000.

### (a) Tax treatment of growth shares

There is no income tax/National Insurance charge if the price paid on acquisition is at least market value. If the price is below market value, a tax charge will arise.

Any such tax will be payable either under self-assessment or PAYE, depending on whether the shares are readily convertible assets. See 14.2.

A key attraction of growth shares is that growth in value will be subject to CGT, and for as long as this is charged at a lower rate than income tax/National Insurance this will make them more attractive from a tax point of view than non-approved options.

### (b) Combining growth shares with EMI options

It is possible for a company to grant EMI options over growth shares (if the EMI eligibility requirements are satisfied). The conditions for claiming entrepreneurs' relief on shares acquired through EMI options are more easily satisfied than where shares are acquired directly, and so it may be easier to ensure a CGT rate on sale of 10%. That said, an EMI option must not be granted if the reason is avoidance of tax, so this route should only be chosen if an option is considered a more effective form of incentive and reward than direct share purchase. For example, the ability to make it a condition of EMI options that the optionholder must remain with the company for a specified period before being eligible to exercise the options might be sufficient to ensure that it is not treated as granted for tax avoidance reasons.

Additionally, because a growth share will have a lower value than an ordinary share, more growth shares can be issued within the EMI statutory limits (see Chapter 12).

### (c) Who is eligible to be issued growth shares?

A company can invite any individual to acquire growth shares.

### (d) Are there any financial limits on growth shares

There are no limitations under tax legislation on the value of growth shares that may be acquired by a single individual or overall by a company.

However, as with any other arrangement involving personal share ownership, the company will wish to place its own overall limit on how many shares may be issued, to limit dilution of other shareholders.

### (e) Corporation tax

Unlike with share options and awards of free shares under a SIP, no corporation tax deduction can be claimed in connection with growth shares.

### (f) Key steps in creating a growth share plan

A company planning to award growth shares should consider the following:

#### (i) What is the company's current value?

It is advisable to take professional advice from an experienced company valuation expert. If the growth share's value threshold is set at a level which is at or below market value (or even a little above it), there will be a tax charge on the individual who acquires them.

#### (ii) On what terms should the growth shares be held?

What happens if the optionholder leaves? Are they required to offer their growth shares for sale, and if so, at what price? Does the price depend on why they are leaving?

Should the shares have voting or dividend rights?

Should other provisions be added to the articles of association at the same time, for example "drag along" and "tag along" under which if the majority shareholder ever wishes to sell to a third party it can require other shareholders also to do so (and entitle them to be bought out).

### (iii) Amend articles of association

It will be necessary to change the company's articles of association. This will require shareholder approval.

### (iv) Subscription agreement

Each employee acquiring growth shares should sign a share subscription agreement with the company, and pay the prescribed purchase price for their shares.

### (v) Communication

Explanation of the scheme is key to its success and it is strongly recommended to prepare a plain English guide for employees acquiring growth shares, perhaps as a Q&A or to arrange a presentation or meeting for participating employees.

### (vi) Internal approval

The company's directors will need to approve the issue of the growth shares. A shareholder resolution will be required to approve changes to the company's articles of association.

### (vii) HMRC registration

A company which issues growth shares must register this with HM Revenue and Customs online by 6 July following the end of the tax year in which the growth shares were first issued.

### (viii) Annual return

A company which has issued growth shares must then complete an HM Revenue and Customs online annual return each year. This must be done following the end of each tax year, by 6 July.

### (g) In summary

Growth shares can work well for a company that wishes to make a one-off award to a small number of employees. However, they can become unwieldy in a company that wishes to involve other employees in share ownership in future years. In the Salkeld Construction example, if the company had wished to make a further award over the same class of growth shares, when the company's value had grown to £8 million, those shares would then have material value because the £5.5 million threshold would have been achieved. This would mean the new holders of growth shares would need to pay a more significant purchase price or otherwise pay income tax/National Insurance on the difference between their purchase price and the shares' value when acquired.

This can be overcome by creating a further class of growth shares with a higher value threshold but may require the company's articles of association to be changed each time to do this.

Making a repeat award of share options is generally going to be far simpler, since there should be no need to change the company's articles of association.

Whilst there may be occasions when growth shares are suitable in an employee-owned company, it is likely that these will be rare and limited to situations where senior leaders are to acquire personal shares and there is no better alternative.

## 14.7  Free or discounted shares

It is possible for employees to acquire shares free or at a purchase price which is less than market value. Chapter 10 looks at how to award free shares under a SIP (which requires all employees to have the opportunity to receive free shares), whereas this part considers awards of free or discounted shares without using a SIP (for example, where only certain employees are to have the opportunity or if a SIP is not considered to be the right solution).

Because of the tax treatment, it is relatively unusual for free or discounted shares to be awarded.

### (a)  How to structure an award of free shares

The Companies Act 2006 prohibits the issue of shares at a price which is less than each share's par (or nominal) value. Where par value is set at a low level (it is not uncommon for a share to have a par value of £0.0001, for example) the amount required to be paid may be negligible, so the shares can be issued directly to employees and are, to all intents and purposes, free.

Where nominal value is higher, it may be necessary to deliver the shares to the employee in a different way. The most common approach involves the company establishing an employee trust, to which it gifts a sum of money. The trust then uses that money to subscribe for new shares (or purchase them from existing shareholders), and then gifts those shares to designated employees.

### (b) How to structure an award of discounted shares

Provided the purchase price per share is at least par value, it will generally be possible for a company to issue shares at a discounted purchase price directly to any participating employees.

### (c) Tax treatment

The award of free shares to an employee or director will give rise to an income tax charge on the shares' value. National Insurance may also be due.

If there is a purchase price but it is less than market value, tax will be payable on the discount.

Any such tax will be payable either under self-assessment or PAYE, depending on whether the shares are readily convertible assets. See 14.2.

### (d) Who is eligible to acquire free or discounted shares?

A company can invite any individual to be given free shares or purchase them for less than their market value.

### (e) Are there any financial limits on the award of free shares?

There are no limitations under tax legislation on the value of shares that may be awarded free or at a discount.

However, any tax liability will increase in line with the number of shares awarded.

### (f) Corporation tax

Subject to meeting the statutory conditions, a company will be able to claim a corporation tax deduction of an amount equal to the value of free shares when they are awarded or, in the case of discounted shares, on the difference between the purchase price and market value when acquired.

### (g) Key steps in issuing free or discounted shares

A company planning to issue ordinary shares should consider the following:

*(i) What is the company's current value?*
Since there will be a tax charge, it is recommended to take professional advice from an experienced company valuation expert.

*(ii) On what terms should they be held?*
The issues discussed in 14.6(f)(ii) should be considered.

*(iii) Amend articles of association?*
The issues discussed in 14.6(f)(iii) should be considered.

*(iv) Subscription or award agreement*
Each employee acquiring free shares by subscription for new shares should enter into a share subscription agreement or letter with the company, and pay the prescribed (nominal) purchase price. If free shares are to be awarded by transfer as a gift from an employee trust, a stock transfer form will be required and it is also common to record the terms in a deed of gift.

In relation to shares which are being bought at a discount, the normal route will be for the employee and the company to sign a share subscription agreement.

*(v) Communication*
As with other forms of employee share ownership, it is strongly recommended to explain clearly to employees how their share ownership arrangement works.

*(vi) Internal approval*
The company's directors will need to approve the issue of the shares. A shareholder resolution will be required to approve any changes to the company's articles of association.

*(vii) HMRC registration*
Any award of free or discounted shares must be registered with HM Revenue and Customs online by 6 July following the end of the tax year in which the shares were acquired.

*(viii) Companies House*
Notification will need to be given to Companies House of any issue of new shares.

*(ix) Annual return*

The company must then complete an HM Revenue and Customs online annual return each year. This must be done following the end of each tax year, by 6 July.

**To recap:**

- This chapter covers these alternative ways in which employees can acquire shares:

    *Non-approved options*
    *Simple purchase of shares*
    *Nil or partly paid shares*
    *Restricted securities*
    *Growth shares*
    *Free or discounted shares*

- Registration with HMRC is required

# 15 Anti-avoidance provision affecting transfers of assets by third parties

## 15.1 Introduction

If it is ever intended to transfer ownership of assets (most likely shares or cash, but this could include any kind of asset) from an employee trust to any employees, it is essential to be aware of the "disguised remuneration" provisions in ITEPA 2003, Part 7A.

This is anti-avoidance legislation, to counter the use of employee trusts to deliver tax free remuneration. It does not prevent the use of tax-advantaged share option or ownership arrangements (EMI, CSOP, SAYE and SIP) where the source of shares is an employee trust, nor does it prevent payment of income tax free bonuses to employees of a company controlled by an employee ownership trust.

But it could affect arrangements where shares, cash or other assets are transferred by a trust (or any other third party) to one or more employees. A key feature of this anti-avoidance legislation is that it can create an income tax charge on an employee before they become owners of particular assets, for example if the trustees of an employee trust make a decision to reserve (or *earmark*) them in the name of a particular employee.

This will not, however, apply where a company transfers or earmarks assets to its employees (or a company in the same group does so), unless it is doing so in a trustee-like capacity. Although the intention of the legislation is to cover certain actions taken by employee benefit trusts, it is sufficiently widely worded to cover actions by other third parties.

This chapter gives an overview only and there is more detail in the underlying legislation. The key purpose of this chapter is to create an awareness of the possible tax risks of allocating any interest or even potential interest in the assets of a trust to any specific employee.

## 15.2 How does it work?

An employee (or director) will become immediately liable to income tax and National Insurance (under PAYE) in either of the situations set out below. These are referred to as *gateways*: if a gateway applies, a tax charge will result unless an exemption is available.

There are two gateways: the ***main gateway*** and the ***close companies gateway***.

### (a) Main gateway

The *main gateway* will apply if:

- *a person (A) is an employee, or former or prospective employee, of another person (B)*
- *there is a **relevant arrangement** to which A is a party or which otherwise relates to A*
- *the relevant arrangement is a means of providing reward, recognition or a loan in connection with A's employment (or former or prospective employment) with B*
- *a **relevant third person** takes a **relevant step** that is connected to the relevant arrangement.*

### (i) Relevant arrangement

A relevant arrangement is wide ranging.

Any arrangement will be regarded as a relevant arrangement if either:

- *it wholly or partly relates to an employee (A) or a person linked to A or*
- *a (or a person linked to A) is a party to the arrangement.*

An ***arrangement*** is intentionally widely worded and includes anything from an understanding to an agreement.

Additionally, the relevant arrangement must in essence be concerned with providing rewards, recognition or loans in connection with A's employment.

### (ii) Relevant third person

A ***relevant third person*** is generally any person who is not one of the following:

- *the employee*

- *the company which employs the employee*
- *any company in the same group as the employer.*

However, if any of the above are acting in a trustee-like capacity, they may also be treated as a relevant third person.

Although the main target of this legislation is employee benefit trusts, which have been extensively used purely as tax planning vehicles[22], others could be considered as a relevant third person, for example an individual shareholder in the employer company or a corporate shareholder which it is not its holding company.

### (iii) Relevant step
The following are regarded as *relevant steps:*

- *earmarking (however informally) or otherwise starting to hold money or any asset with a view to using it to benefit an employee (including family members and associates, a cohabiting unmarried partner or any other person chosen by any person in those categories)*
- *making a payment, including a loan, or transferring an asset, to a person who is liable to pay income tax (a taxable recipient)*
- *making any asset available for a taxable recipient.*


**Sowerby Engineering Limited**

**The main gateway**
In this example we show where each of the above key terms apply.

Sowerby Engineering **(B)** is partly owned by an employee benefit trust **(relevant third party)**, which also holds some cash. The trustees lend £50,000 **(relevant step)** to their chief technology officer, Ash Khatri **(A)**. The loan is a **relevant arrangement.** Although the terms of the loan state

---

[22] As other parts of this book explain,  employee benefit trusts can play an entirely proper and useful role as a key part of a company's employee ownership. But in the past they have also been put to a less wholesome purpose: providing cash rewards to key employees, often in large amounts, free of income tax and National Insurance.  An employee benefit trust can be likened to a mechanical digger: it can be used to dig the foundations for a new school (good) or to ramraid an ATM machine (not so good).

that it is to be repaid within five years, an income tax and National Insurance liability arises immediately on £50,000. Eventual repayment of the loan will not enable these taxes to be refunded.

The trustees also decide to reserve 10,000 shares for its chief executive, Hannah Terrett (**A**), which have a value of £70,000. It is not immediately clear how, when and on what terms Hannah may eventually acquire full ownership of these shares. This is also a **relevant step** and is likely also to be regarded as a **relevant arrangement** and so will also be covered by the disguised remuneration legislation, so income tax and National Insurance will be payable on their value

## (b) Close companies gateway

This is very similar to the *main gateway* but with one important difference, which is that the employer (B) must provide finance.

It will apply where:

- *a person (A) is an employee or director of B and holds, or has in the past three years held, shares comprising at least 5% of B*
- *B is a close company (broadly, this means controlled by no more than five shareholders)*
- *there is a **relevant arrangement** to which A is a party or which otherwise relates to A*
- *the relevant arrangement is (in broad terms) a way of providing loans to A or persons linked with A and a main purpose is avoidance of certain taxes*
- *B (in broad terms) funds the arrangement (for example by making a payment to the relevant third person (see below)) – this is called a **relevant transaction***
- *a **relevant third person** takes a **relevant step** that relates to the same asset which was the subject of the relevant transaction.*

### A66 Acoustics Limited

#### The close companies gateway
A66 Acoustics (**B**) is a close company, being majority owned by an employee benefit trust.

A66 lends £100,000 to a second employee benefit trust, which does not hold shares in A66. The reason for the loan is to enable that trust to lend the money  to the company's chief executive, Monica Alfonsi **(A)**, who holds a 5% shareholding. The reason for structuring the loan through the trust, rather than the company making the loan directly to Monica,  is to avoid the company paying corporation tax on the loan as if it were a distribution to her.

The loan to the trust is a **relevant transaction** and the arrangement to make a loan to Monica is a **relevant arrangement.**  The trust is a **relevant third party** and its **relevant step** is its loan to Monica.

This arrangement will result in a charge to income tax and National Insurance and eventual repayment of the loan will not enable these taxes to be refunded.

Would this arrangement not have been caught by the main gateway? Perhaps it would, but the company might then have argued that the loan to Monica was being made by reason of her status as a shareholder rather than as an employee, which if successful would have meant no tax charge.

## 15.3  When it does not apply

These anti-avoidance arrangements will not apply (under either gateway) in certain circumstances, which are considered below.

### (a)  Arrangements for individual employee share ownership

#### (i)  The core exceptions

Relevant steps taken in any of the following situations will not result in a tax charge:

- *those taken under an EMI, CSOP, SAYE or SIP tax advantaged share scheme (see further below)*
- *those taken to grant share options (but a charge may apply if shares are specifically earmarked to satisfy the exercise of options)*
- *those taken to provide an employee with restricted securities that are subject to a risk of forfeiture which will fall away within five years*
- *those resulting in an income tax charge under various tax provisions relating to employment-related securities and options.*

The above are potentially the most relevant to employee-owned companies.

## *(ii)  Additional points*

If a company takes a relevant step for the general purpose of acquiring, holding and delivering shares under a CSOP, SAYE or SIP scheme, it is not connected with tax avoidance and the total number of shares held by the relevant third person (and any other persons) is no greater than the number which might reasonably be expected to be required for that scheme over the next ten years, no tax charge will apply.

A similar exception applies in relation to EMI options.

## (b)  Other exceptions

Additional relevant steps which will not lead to a tax charge include:

- *those taken under a registered pension scheme*
- *arrangements to provide death in service, life policies and other benefits*
- *those connected with some employee car ownership schemes*
- *earmarking of money or assets for awards to employees of deferred remuneration (subject to certain conditions)*
- *certain loans to facilitate the exercise of share options (which must be paid within 40 days).*

## 15.4  Leaving shares to employees in a will

A shareholder may, as part of their plans for ownership succession, wish to leave shares to one or more employees in their will. Could the disguised remuneration rules apply, so that a tax charge arises on the employees concerned as soon as the will has been signed?

It is likely that leaving shares in a will is going to be treated as earmarking (one of the relevant steps).

The key question is whether there is a relevant arrangement which (paraphrasing the legislation) is wholly or partly to provide or concerned with providing rewards, recognition or loans in connection with employment.

If the bequest is made because the employee to whom it is made is a close friend of the shareholder, it is arguable that it does not relate to the employment and so is not caught by the rules.

However, if the bequest is made to several employees, this argument is likely to be harder to support.

## 15.5  How is the tax calculated?

Tax is generally payable on the higher of the market value of the assets subject to the relevant step and the cost of providing the benefit.

It is collected under PAYE irrespective of whether the assets are readily convertible.

### Crosby Architects Limited

Crosby Architects is 80% owned by an employee ownership trust and 20% owned by the company's founder, Alex Crosby.

The trust deed contains a provision which says that if the trust were ever to sell its shares, the sale proceeds would be distributed to employees on a same terms basis that takes into account their salaries.

Also, Alex has granted EMI options to one individual director, over half her shareholding.

Although it would be possible to determine from time to time the proportion of any sale proceeds that an employee would receive if the trust were ever to distribute sale proceeds, this provision will not be treated as subject to the disguised remuneration legislation. There has been no relevant step.

The EMI options will not be subject to the legislation either. The number of shares held by Alex to satisfy the EMI option grant is the same as the number granted (Alex's other shares are not counted as they are not part of the arrangement for the grant of EMI options).

### To recap:
- Awards of assets to an employee by a third party, including a promise or indication that an asset will be transferred or even an informal "earmarking", can give rise to an immediate income tax charge on that asset's value.
- This applies even though the employee has not received ownership of that asset.

- The main gateway:
  - *Employee, former or prospective employee (A) of another person (B)*
  - *Relevant arrangement involving A (widely defined)*
  - *Its purpose is providing reward to A*
  - *Relevant third person (third party) takes relevant step (earmarking, making loan, making an asset available).*
- The close companies gateway:
  - *Similar to main gateway but employer must provide finance*
  - *Relevant arrangement is way of providing a loan to A*
  - *Employer (B) funds the relevant arrangement*
  - *Relevant step is a loan to A.*
- Exceptions include certain arrangements for individual employee share ownership.

# 16 Legal, regulatory and other tax points

## 16.1 Introduction

Depending on how employee ownership is structured in a given company, a number of legal and regulatory requirements might potentially apply.

Most of these will only be relevant for a company which operates individual share ownership (which will usually run alongside ownership of a controlling or significant shareholding by an employee trust). However, the first requirement considered below contains elements which apply both where there is combined trust and individual ownership and where is only trust ownership.

## 16.2 Financial Services and Markets Act 2000 (FSMA)

### (a) Financial promotion

The main provision of FSMA which is potentially relevant to any arrangement under which shares are offered to individuals is the *restriction on financial promotion*.

In short, any offer to individuals to acquire shares or options will be regarded as a financial promotion if it is made in the course of business. Unless an exemption is available, that offer must be issued or approved by a person authorised under FSMA.

### (i) Employee share scheme exemption

In practice, it would often be prohibitively expensive and complex to engage an authorised person to approve any offer of shares to employees. Companies wishing to offer shares to their employees (or to any of them) will generally be able to use an exemption which applies to communications in connection with an *employee share scheme*, which is defined as:

*"arrangements made or to be made by [company] C or by a person in the same group as C to enable or facilitate:*
- *transactions in [certain investments] between or for the benefit of:*
  - *the bona fide employees or former employees of C or of another member of the same group as C;*
  - *the wives, husbands, widows, widowers or children or step-children under the age of eighteen of such employees or former employees; or*

- *the holding of those investments by, or for the benefit of, such persons".*

This exception will generally enable offers of shares to be made by a company to its employees without the offer having to be approved by an authorised person, in relation to shares in that company or any other company in the same group as the employer company.

### (ii) Limits to the employee share scheme exception

There are two potential wrinkles. What happens where shares or options:

- *are not offered to employees (for example individuals who are directors but not employees, or self-employed consultants)?Or,*
- *are offered by an employee trust?*

The exemption will not apply to offers made to non-employees. It may not be straightforward to identify an alternative exception, so if an offer is made which is neither approved by an authorised person nor the subject of an exception, a breach of the financial promotion restriction may occur.

An offer of shares or options made by trustees of an employee trust may not fall within the employee share scheme exception, because the offer must be made by a company in the same group as the employer company. For this reason, an employee trust intending to offer shares or options to employees will often have a corporate trustee which is in the same group as the employer company.

### (b) The general prohibition

FSMA also prohibits the carrying on, by way of business, of several regulated activities relating to a range of different kinds of investments.

These include dealing in shares and options, giving financial advice, holding investments for others and investment management.

In the context of an individual employee share ownership arrangement, the most likely situation where regulated activities might be carried on is where an employee trust acquires, holds and then makes awards over shares. Generally, however, unless it is doing this as a professional trustee, it is unlikely that it will be regarded as doing so "by way of business".

Here, "professional trustee" means a single corporate trustee providing trustee services for a fee (or, unusually, it could also mean a group of individual trustees who are doing so). It would not mean a single corporate trustee which had some paid independent trustee-directors and some other trustee-directors who were unpaid or paid only a small fee, nor would it mean a group of individual trustees where the same payment arrangements applied.

## 16.3  Offering shares to employees – could a prospectus be required?

In some situations, a company offering shares to its employees will need to produce a prospectus containing extensive and detailed information about the company, the shares being offered and other related matters.

These requirements derive from the EU Prospective Directive.

### (a)  When is a prospectus required?

The starting point is that a public offer of transferable securities in the UK must be made through a prospectus approved by the Financial Conduct Authority.

An offer of free shares will not generally require a prospectus.

Offers of share options are generally not subject to the requirement either, because they are normally personal to the optionholder and not transferable.

### (b)  Exceptions

Offers to purchase shares may require a prospectus but only if:

- *the offer is made to 150 or more employees in each EU member state (remember that this law derives from the European Union), and*
- *the total consideration under the offer is 8 million Euros or greater.*

For most employee-owned companies offering shares to their employees, it will be possible to avoid the requirement to produce a prospectus by applying one of the above de minimis exceptions.

## 16.4 Loans to employees: Consumer Credit Act

If an individual receives a loan to finance their purchase of shares, or if they are simply allowed to defer the date when they pay for shares they have acquired (nil or partly paid shares – see Chapter 14), the consumer credit regime may apply. Originating in the Consumer Credit Act 1974, this now forms part of the Financial Services and Markets Act 2000.

A company may make a loan to an individual to fund their acquisition of shares at the time they are exercising share options, or where an individual is simply taking up an invitation to purchase shares.

In any circumstances where it is proposed to make a loan or extend credit, the impact of consumer credit laws should be considered.

### (a) Does the consumer credit regime apply?

The first question to consider is whether credit is provided.

The issue by a company of nil or partly paid shares will not involve the company extending credit under the consumer credit regime, so long as the terms of the deferred payment are such that the individual acquiring the shares will only owe a debt to the company if and when it makes a call for payment of the purchase price.

This must be differentiated from shares issued as fully paid shares but where the obligation to pay the subscription price for them is deferred. Here, the regime may apply because the individual acquiring the shares has taken on a contractual obligation to pay the deferred amount at a future point.

The making of a loan to purchase shares, where funds pass to the purchaser, who then uses that loan to pay for the shares, is likely to fall within the regime.

### (b) What is the impact of the regime?

If a person carries out a *regulated activity .... by way of business*, they will need to be authorised by the Financial Conduct Authority.

## (i)  Regulated activity

The making of a loan (or the extending of credit) through a *regulated credit agreement* will be a regulated activity, unless it is made under an *exempt agreement*.

A *regulated credit agreement* means (in summary) any agreement between an individual (A) and any other person (B) under which B provides A with credit.

There are a number of types of agreement that will be regarded as *exempt agreements*. In the context of credit provided for employees to acquire shares, only the following are likely to be relevant:

- *certain agreements, called borrower-lender-supplier agreements (broadly, an agreement to finance the supply of goods or services by the lender), where the credit is repayable in four or fewer payments over less than 12 months and no interest is charged;*
- *if the borrower is an individual with income of at least £150,000 and/or net assets of not less than £500,000 (the "high net worth individual" exemption); and*
- *low cost credit arrangements. here, the key requirements are:*
  - *the credit is offered to an employee in the course of their employment*
  - *interest is not more than 1% above base rate and cannot be increased*
  - *the arrangement must be a borrower-lender agreement (this generally means the purpose of the credit must be to enable the borrower to acquire goods or services from a person other than the lender).*
  - *if the lender is also the supplier of the shares (for example, where a company provides credit to enable employees to subscribe for shares in the company), the credit will not be supplied under a borrower-lender agreement, and so this exemption will not apply.*

## (ii)  By way of business

Even if the provision of loans is not a company's main business, it may be regarded as providing credit *by way of business*.

If a company is providing credit with a view to making a profit, or if doing so has a material impact on its wider business activities, it is likely that it will be regarded as doing so by way of business.

Factors which should be taken into account include:

- *how often credit is provided*
- *whether there is a commercial element*
- *the scale of the activity and the proportion the activity bears to other, non-regulated, activities*
- *the nature of the activity.*

### Carlin Associates Limited

Carlin Associates is 100% owned by an employee ownership trust. It wishes to put in place an arrangement under which all of its employees will be able to borrow money from the company to purchase shares, paying a market value price.

It has not done this previously and has no plans to do so again in the future, the loan arrangement being regarded as a one-off event.

The total maximum amount of the loans will, in aggregate, be no more than 2% of the company's annual revenues. The loans will be interest free.

In this situation it is unlikely that it will be regarded as providing credit by way of business.

In the following year, further loans are offered to employees as part of a new plan to enable all staff to acquire shares on an annual basis. The loans are to start bearing interest at base rate plus 4%. These new factors may have the effect that the company is now providing credit by way of business.

## (c) Authorisation by the Financial Conduct Authority
What are the consequences of failure to comply?

Where authorisation is required but not obtained:

- *loans will be unenforceable (unless the FCA gives permission in writing for enforcement), and*
- *the provider of the credit will have committed a criminal offence.*

## (d) Other consequences of a loan being made under a regulated credit agreement
Irrespective of whether authorisation by the FCA is required, it may be necessary to go through various formalities as part of providing credit to an individual to enable them to acquire shares.

A credit agreement which falls within the definition of a ***non-commercial agreement*** will not be subject to these requirements. A non-commercial agreement is a regulated agreement (under the Consumer Credit Act 1974) that is not made by the creditor in the course of a consumer credit business carried on by him. So for all companies other than those which operate a consumer credit business, these formalities will not apply.

Where they do apply:

- *the borrower must be supplied with a document setting out certain pre-contract information;*
- *the credit agreement must then contain, in a clear and concise manner, information including: name and address of borrower and lender; the type of agreement; duration of the credit; amount of the credit; interest rate; total amount payable by the borrower; the timing and amount of repayments;*
- *a fourteen day withdrawal period must be allowed; and*
- *the borrower must be provided with an annual statement.*

Where credit is provided to employees under non-commercial agreements, it is arguably still good practice to ensure that there is a written agreement with each employee, that the key terms of the loan are clearly set out in a separate statement and, where possible, a "cooling off" or withdrawal period is allowed. These are not legal requirements but will help to ensure that employees are clear about the obligations they are taking on.

## 16.5  Loans to employees: income tax relief on interest

An employee taking out a loan to purchase ordinary shares in a close company may claim income tax relief on the interest if:

- *they hold a material interest in the company (broadly 5% or more); or*
- *they work for the greater part of their time in the management of conduct of the company, between the date when the shares are acquired and payment of interest.*

Income tax relief is also available on a loan to acquire shares in an employee-controlled company (see 14.4(a)).

## 16.6  Internal approvals for issue of new shares

Where a company is to issue new shares to employees, it will need to ensure that this is properly approved. As a minimum, this will mean approval by the company's directors and may also require shareholder approval.

### (a)  Director approval

Every time a company issues new shares, or grants options to acquire shares, the company's directors must give their formal approval. This should be recorded in a formal minute of the directors' meeting at which the approval is given. Alternatively, if it is difficult to arrange a meeting and the company's articles of association and/or shareholder agreement allows, approval can be given in the form of a resolution signed by all directors.

### (b)  Shareholder approval

It may also be necessary to obtain shareholder approval to the issue of new shares. Where the step being taken is the grant of options (so the actual issue of shares will not take place until later in time, if the options are exercised), any necessary shareholder approval could be deferred until the time of option exercise. However, to avoid the risk of shareholders ultimately deciding not to give the necessary approval, it is recommended to obtain it at the same time as the options are granted. This also avoids the risk of overlooking the need for approval at the time of option exercise, when the need for it may have been forgotten.

The need for shareholder approval may arise in up to four principal ways. To establish whether any of these apply, it will be necessary to review the company's articles of association and any shareholders' agreement.

### (i)  Directors' authority to issue new shares under the Companies Act

Have the shareholders authorised the directors to issue new shares under the Companies Act 2006?

Under this legislation (CA 2006, sections 550 and 551), directors may only issue new shares if authorised by shareholders.

There is an exception for shares to be issued under an *employees' share scheme*. However, this will not be of use where shares are to be issued to non-employees (including directors who are not employees and self-employed consultants) and the exception will be overridden by any requirement in the company's articles of association or shareholders' agreement requiring shareholder authority.

An employees' share scheme is defined as:

*"a scheme for encouraging or facilitating the holding of shares in or debentures of a company by or for the benefit of:*

- *The bona fide employees or former employees of the company, its subsidiaries, its holding company or any subsidiary of such holding company; and*
- *The spouses, civil partners, surviving spouses, surviving civil partners or minor children or step-children of such employees or former employees".*

How do you show that you have an employees' share scheme? Best recommended practice is to have a formal document setting out the parameters of the arrangements under which employees may acquire shares. This need not be long or detailed. Alternatively, any agreement between the company and the employee which sets out the terms under which they are acquiring shares (this can include an option agreement) may be sufficient, so long as there is a possibility that further share awards or option grants may follow in the future.

A scheme that allows for shares or options to be awarded to non-employees, as well as employees, risks not being an employees' share scheme.

### (ii) Directors' authority to issue new shares under its articles or shareholder agreement
Check each of these documents carefully to see if shareholder authority (or the authority of any particular shareholder or percentage of shareholders) is needed before any new shares can be issued. Some companies have their own requirements for obtaining

shareholder authority for the issue or new shares, rather than relying on the Companies Act provisions referred to above.

### (iii) Shareholders' right of first refusal under the Companies Act

Existing shareholders may have a right of pre-emption (first refusal) under section 561. Where this is present, the company will not be able to issue new shares until those shares have first been offered to existing shareholders in proportion to the size of their holdings. The purpose of the legislation is to give existing shareholders the opportunity to prevent their shareholdings from being diluted (in percentage terms) by subscribing for new shares.

This right will exist unless the company's articles specifically exclude it (or shareholders have passed a special resolution to do so) or if the articles contain separate equivalent rights.

As with directors' authority to issue new shares (see above), this statutory pre-emption provision does not apply to the issue of shares under an *employees' share scheme*, so there will be no statutory pre-emption rights on the issue of shares to employees as long as an employees' share scheme exists. This exception does not apply to shares issued to non-employees, as with the exception applying to directors' authority.

### (iv) Shareholders' right of first refusal: company's own pre-emption provisions

It is common for companies to disapply the statutory pre-emption right and replace it with their own in their articles of association. Where this is done, there is no automatic employees' share scheme exemption, so unless the company has included its own it will be necessary either to comply with the pre-emption provisions (unlikely to be practical, perhaps unless the company has a single existing shareholder or a very small number of shareholders) or ask shareholders to disapply them in accordance with the articles of association.

**To recap:**

- Financial Services and Markets Act 2000 regulates *financial promotion* of investments, which could apply to offers of shares to employees.
- However, there is an *employee share scheme* exemption (but it only applies to employees, so take care where shares or options are offered to non-employees).
- General prohibition on *regulated activities.*
- But this only applies to activities *"by way of business"*.
- Offering shares to employees – prospectus may be required but exceptions mean that many smaller companies will not be subject to this requirement.
- Consumer credit regime may apply to loans to employees. Availability of exemptions will depend on the circumstances.
- Awards of shares or options by a company generally need to be approved by directors. Shareholder approval may also be required.

# 17 General Data Protection Regulation (GDPR) and Data Protection Act

A detailed analysis of this area of law is beyond the scope of this book. However, certain practical points are discussed below.

An employer will hold personal data as part of operating any kind of employee share ownership or option scheme, so it will be important to be clear as to the impact of the data protection regulatory framework.

## 17.1    Consent to process personal data)

It is recommended that the rules of any employee share scheme contain a data privacy notice which complies with GDPR, and that each participating employee be supplied with this notice. This replaces previous practice of implying consent pre-GDPR.

For existing schemes which do not already contain this wording, it is recommended that scheme rules be amended to contain a data privacy notice.

## 17.2    Sending personal data to the trustee of an employee trust

There may be occasions when it is necessary for an employer company to send to the trustees of an employee trust personal data relating to employees. This could arise, for example, where the trustees propose to transfer shares to employees individually or where, following the sale of the company by the trustees, they plan to distribute sale proceeds to employees as beneficiaries of the trust.

### (a)     Need for contract

In any such situation, there should be a clear contract between the company (as *data controller*)) and the trustees (as *data processor*)) that imposes obligations on the trustees. These are likely to include keeping a record of:  the trustees' name(s) and contact details; the trustees' data protection officer (if it has one); the categories of processing to be carried out; and the data protection measures put in place by the trustees.

This requirement does not apply where there are fewer than 250 employees unless *one of the following* applies:
- *the processing to be carried out is likely to result in risk for the rights and freedoms of any employee*
- *the processing is not occasional*
- *the processing includes special categories of personal data relating to criminal convictions and offences.*

## (c)    Company needs to identify a lawful basis
For the company to send personal data to trustees, it will need to identify a lawful basis for doing so.

Possible lawful bases include:
- *the processing is necessary for the performance of a contract or to take steps at the request of the data subject prior to entering into a contract or*
- *the processing is necessary for the legitimate interests of the company (data controller).*

Which, if either, of these will apply will depend on the circumstances.

**To recap:**
- Recommended that rules of any employee share scheme include data privacy notice and that this be supplied to participant.
- Contract often needed where data is to be sent to an employee trust, but exception for company with fewer than 250 employees.
- Company also needs to identify a lawful basis for doing so.

# 18  Phantom shares

A company wishing to provide for long term employee reward in a way which does not involve them acquiring shares personally could consider establishing a *phantom share scheme.*

## (a)  How phantom share schemes work

In its purest form, a phantom share scheme works exactly in the way its name suggests. A worked example follows:

### Clifford Transport Limited: phantom share scheme

Clifford Transport, a haulage and logistics company, is 100% owned by an employee ownership trust. It wishes to set up a long-term financial reward arrangement for its directors. The trustees' policy is not to distribute shares to individual employees, so it is decided to establish an arrangement which rewards directors as if they held shares.

### *Terms of the scheme*
Each director (Mohammed, Alison and Richard) is allocated 30 units in the scheme. Each unit entitles its holder to a payment equal to 0.1% of any growth in the company's value over the next five years (so each participant is potentially entitled to a payment of 3% of growth).

The units "vest" as to six units per participant in each of the five years following the award. This means that if any participant leaves in that period (unless a "bad leaver") they will be entitled to a payment based on the number of units vested and the growth in company value over the period until they left. The company reserves the right to defer making that payment until the five-year period has been completed.

A "bad leaver" is a participant who leaves voluntarily or is fairly dismissed due to misconduct or inability to do their job.

The Company has a value of £5 million when the awards are made.

### *After the five years*
The company's value has grown to £8 million. Each participant apart from Richard is paid a cash sum of £90,000 before tax.

*Why is Richard excluded?*

### *Richard*
Richard resigned two years into the scheme. He was therefore a bad leaver and forfeited any rights to receive a payment.

Had he left other than as a bad leaver (for example, because of ill-health) he would have been entitled to a part payment. For example, if he left in those circumstances and the company's value at that time was £6 million, he would have been entitled to a payment of £30,000 (£1 million growth x 3%). The company would have the right to defer making this payment until the full five years had passed (but might, if it had sufficient cash, exercise discretion to do so earlier taking into account Richard's circumstances).

## (b) Taxation

A phantom share scheme is a form of long term cash bonus. Any amounts paid to participants will therefore be subject to income tax and National Insurance and PAYE will apply.

Tax should only be due when payments are actually made. However, care is needed if the person operating the scheme is not the company but a third party (such as an employee benefit trust), as an initial award of a right to participate could give rise to a tax charge even though any payment will only be made some time in the future (if ever). See Chapter 15.

## (c) Eligibility

A company operating a phantom share scheme can select any employees it wishes for participation. In practice, participation tends to be limited to senior leadership team members but there is no reason in principle why all employees should not be involved if it makes commercial sense to do so.

## (d) Are then any financial limits?

No financial limits operate. However, unlike a reward arrangement involving shares (which creates no cash obligation on the company, unless it has taken the bold step of guaranteeing to buy shares back from shareholders), it does involve a definite commitment to pay cash sums at a future date. The size of this commitment is indeterminate when the scheme begins; it will only be known at the end of the scheme period (five years in the previous example). It is therefore recommended that a company operating a phantom share scheme, model its anticipated cash and distributable profits against a range of different performance scenarios.

It is also worth considering whether the scheme should allow for any payouts under it to be made in instalments after the end of the period over which company performance is measured.

### (e) Corporation tax

A company making payments under a phantom share scheme to its participating employees will be able to claim a deduction against corporation tax.

### (f) Key steps in establishing a phantom share scheme

A company planning to establish a phantom share scheme should consider the following:

### (i) What is the purpose of the scheme and who is it for?

Why is the scheme being established and how does it link to the company's strategy or business plan? If the company's aim is to achieve long term growth rather than short term profit, any measure of performance and how this is linked to reward for participants will need to reflect that.

Clarity is needed about who is to participate. Will all the company's employees engage with a reward scheme linked to long term performance or should they instead be paid an annual bonus or profit share, leaving participation in the phantom share scheme to the senior leadership?

### (ii) What should be the terms of the scheme?

Some key questions here are:
- What is the performance measure and over what period?
- How should leavers be treated?
- Will the company be able to afford any eventual payments?

### (iii) Communication

As with any form of share ownership scheme, clear communication to participants about the scheme's purpose and how it works is essential, as is further communication through the life of the scheme. The scheme's success will depend on participants knowing how their company is performing, what steps (if any) may be needed to improve it and the level of reward that it is on track to deliver.

## (iv) Internal approval

The establishment of a phantom share scheme should be approved by the company's board of directors. In a company that is majority owned by an employee trust, the trustees' approval would generally also be sought.

**To recap:**
- Phantom schemes do not involve real shares.
- Payments are subject to income tax and National Insurance but are corporation tax deductible.
- No financial limits.
- Need for cashflow planning to ensure company will have sufficient funds for eventual payments.
- Need to consider treatment of leavers, and how performance is measured.

# 19  Corporation tax relief

This chapter looks at the interaction between employee ownership and corporation tax, specifically when and how a company can claim a deduction against corporation tax.

## 19.1  What is deductible against corporation tax?

The following are the principal situations where a company can claim a corporation tax deduction. In each case, the deduction is claimed by the company which employs the employee(s) (so in a group of companies, this will generally be a subsidiary rather than the holding company):

- *gains made on the exercise of options*
- *where an employee acquires shares directly, the difference between the price paid and their value at the time of acquisition*
- *cash payments in connection with cancellation of share options*
- *the lifting of restrictions on shares*
- *awards of free or matching shares under a SIP*
- *the cost of establishing certain types of employee share scheme.*

## 19.2  What are the requirements for claiming a corporation tax deduction?

For a company to claim a corporation tax deduction in respect of gains made on exercise of options or an award of shares, the principal requirements are:

### (a)  Employment and business

The employment of the person acquiring shares or exercising options must be in relation to a business carried on by the employing company, and that company must be subject to corporation tax on its profits.

### (b)  The shares

The shares acquired must:

- *be ordinary shares, fully paid up and not redeemable, and*
- *be in an independent company (that is, not controlled by another company), or otherwise in a listed company or (broadly) in a company controlled by a listed company.*

Where a company is controlled by the corporate trustee of an employee trust (including an employee ownership trust), it will not be regarded as independent and so a deduction will not be available.

### (c) The company

The shares acquired must be (broadly) in the employer company or the employer company's parent company. (There are additional rules allowing shares in a company which is a member of a consortium).

The shares acquired do not necessarily need to be new issue shares. For example, the shares' source could be the employer company, its parent, an employee trust or an existing shareholder.

### (d) The employee's tax position

The employee must:

- *be subject to income tax in respect of the share award or option gain, or*
- *be able to claim relief from income tax because the options are EMI, CSOP or SAYE.*

### (e) When can a deduction be claimed?

Corporation tax relief is given for the accounting period in which the shares are acquired/options are exercised.

### (f) What is the amount of the corporation tax deduction?

The employer company will be able to claim a deduction for the difference between the amount paid for the shares and their market value at the date when they are acquired.

**Lune E Bikes Limited**

***Background***

Lune E Bikes manufactures and distributes electric bicycles. Its financial period runs to 31 December. The following events take place in November.

Sumati exercises unapproved options granted to her four years previously. She exercises options over 10,000 shares, paying £1 per share. Each share is now valued at £5.

Andrew exercises EMI options granted to him at the same time as Sumati received her unapproved options (hers were not EMI because she was not a full-time employee when they were granted). He exercises options over the same number of shares at the same price.

Maria does not hold any options but is invited to purchase shares directly. She pays £1 per share for 2,000 shares.

The various conditions for claiming a corporation deduction in relation to the option exercises and share acquisitions are met.

**Amount of deduction**
Lune E Bikes can claim a deduction against corporation tax for £88,000 in respect of its profits for the period to 31 December in which the shares are acquired, that is:

- Sumati's option gains of £40,000
- Andrew's option gains of £40,000
- In relation to the shares acquired by Maria, the £8,000 difference between the price she paid for her shares and their value when acquired.

## 19.3 Exchange of options on a takeover
If:

- *an option is granted which, if exercised, would result in a corporation tax deduction, and*
- *the company whose shares are subject to the option comes under the control of another company, and*
- *the optionholder agrees to release his options in exchange for the grant of new options in the acquiror (or another qualifying company),*

the employer company retains the right to claim corporation tax relief on any eventual option gains if the option is subsequently exercised.

## 19.4 Cash cancellation of share options
If an employee agrees to surrender their options in return for a cash payment, the employer company can claim a corporation tax deduction for the amount of the payment that is subject to income tax (in the vast majority of cases, this will be all of it), as long as the payment is made wholly and exclusively for the purposes of the company's trade and is not of a capital nature.

## 19.5 Restricted shares

Where shares acquired are restricted shares and any of the restrictions are lifted, a corporation tax deduction can be claimed. The amount is the same as the amount subject to income tax.

## 19.6 Special rules for awards of free and matching shares under a SIP

There are separate rules governing tax deductions for the cost of providing shares under a SIP. These are considered in 10.13.

## 19.7 Costs of establishing employee share schemes

A statutory tax deduction is available for the cost of setting up a CSOP, SAYE and SIP employee share scheme.

There is no statutory deduction for the cost of setting up an unapproved or EMI option scheme, or any other form of share scheme. Accordingly, a deduction can only be claimed if, under general principles, it can be shown that the expenditure was incurred wholly and exclusively for the benefit of the company's trade. HM Revenue and Customs' view is that this will not be possible and therefore it should instead be treated as capital expenditure.

## 19.8 Costs of establishing an employee trust

There is no statutory corporation tax deduction for the cost of setting up an employee benefit trust or employee ownership trust and it is generally unlikely that HM Revenue and Customs would allow a deduction under general principles.

## 19.9 A company's contributions to an employee trust

Once a company has established an employee trust, it would be common for the company to fund it through gifted capital contributions. For example, where an employee ownership trust has been established as part of an ownership succession plan, it will generally be funded in this way.

Although there are two circumstances in which a deduction can be claimed for contributions to an employee trust, in practice they will rarely apply. It will not therefore be possible for the company to claim these payments as a deductible expense, so it will need to be confident that its post-corporation tax profits will be sufficient to cover the trust's obligations to pay purchase price instalments.

These circumstances, and the reason they generally will not apply, are explained below.

First, a deduction will be available to the extent that the trust makes payments to beneficiaries which are income taxable. In practice, it is more likely that payments will be made directly by the company itself, which will be able to claim its own corporation tax deduction. One possible exception is where a trust, having disposed of its shares, distributes the net proceeds to beneficiaries. In that situation it is possible that a corporation tax deduction may be available but it will be necessary to demonstrate that the payment was made wholly and exclusively for the benefit of the company's trade.

Second, a deduction is available if the trust awards shares to employees, or grants options to them which are subsequently exercised. However, the statutory deduction explained earlier in this chapter will take precedence.

**To recap:**
- Deductions available for:
  - *share option gains*
  - *discounts on share purchase price/free shares*
  - *SIPs: free and matching shares*
  - *Cash cancellation payments in relation to options given up*
  - *The lifting of restrictions*
  - *Costs of establishing some employee share schemes.*
- Deduction is for employer company.
- Does not apply to options/shares for non-employees.

# 20 Registration, continuing administration and accounting

Depending on what new share ownership arrangements a company has created, it may be necessary to notify HM Revenue and Customs about them, and in some cases to provide HMRC with annual updates to ensure that they are aware of any changes.

There may also be specific administration or record keeping requirements.

## 20.1 Employee trust

The guidance below applies both to employee ownership trusts and employee benefit trusts.

### (a) Offshore trust

HM Revenue and Customs must be notified of the formation of any trust which is not resident in the United Kingdom, within three months of its establishment.

This is done by sending to HM Revenue and Customs a "Section 218 notice"[23], in the form of a letter providing the name and address of the company which has established the trust and of the trustees.

### (b) Trust registration service

it may be necessary to register an employee trust with HM Revenue and Customs under the Money Laundering, Terrorist Financing and Transfer of Funds (Information on the Payer) Regulations 2017.

Registration is required if the trust is liable to pay any of the following taxes:
Income tax
Capital gains tax
Inheritance tax
Stamp duty land tax
Scottish land and buildings transaction tax
Stamp duty reserve tax.

---

[23] This refers to of the Inheritance Tax Act 1984, section 218

This requirement may be extended to cover a wider range of trusts, including those not liable to pay any of the above taxes.

### (c) Other notification to HM Revenue and Customs

HM Revenue and Customs should be separately notified of the formation of any new employee trust, and an annual trust tax return completed.

Many employee trusts will not have any taxable income and it is possible that after a period of the trust producing nil returns HM Revenue and Customs may agree that no further return is needed until an event occurs giving rise to a tax liability which needs to be reported in a tax return.

If an employee trust has a corporate trustee, that company should also be registered with HM Revenue and Customs and should produce its own corporation tax return. This will generally be a nil return as the trustee company is unlikely to make a taxable profit in its own right.

### (d) Record keeping requirement

Under the same Regulations, an employee trust will be required to keep a record of the following:

- *the company which established it;*
- *the trustees, including a contact address;*
- *the trust's beneficiaries;*
- *any individual who has control of the trust; and*
- *names of any advisers providing legal, financial or tax advice to the trust.*

The recording of beneficiaries can generally be covered by reference to how a beneficiary is defined (e.g. *"beneficiaries are all employees with twelve months' service or more"*). However, if the trustees resolve to confer benefit on any particular individual, the records will also need to include that information.

## 20.2  Employee share schemes

HM Revenue and Customs also require the registration of employee share schemes, and annual notification of information about each scheme. Precise registration requirements depend on the scheme concerned.

## (a) EMI options

Within 92 days of the creation of a *new EMI scheme* (which means any arrangement under which employees may be, or have been, granted EMI options – so a new EMI scheme will be created when a company first decides to grant EMI options), HM Revenue and Customs must be notified.

This is done online using their Employment Related Securities online filing system. It is recommended that registration be started as soon as possible.

Where the company over whose shares the option has been granted is not part of a group, that company must register the EMI scheme. It will need to operate PAYE to do so. Where there is a group of companies, registration can be done by any group company with a PAYE reference but it will normally be the employer company.

It is not possible for a company's adviser (its *agent* in HM Revenue and Customs language) to register the scheme; the company must do this itself.

Once the EMI scheme has been registered, there is a second stage: notifying the grant of EMI options under the scheme. This can be done either by the company or its agent.

Both these steps must be completed within 92 days of the grant of EMI options.

Any subsequent grant of EMI options must also be registered within 92 days of the date of grant, but there is no need to repeat registration of the scheme itself.

It is recommended to take a screenshot of each part of the registration process (both of the scheme and the option grants) as this is the only way to keep a record of what has been submitted.

Failure to comply with these requirements means that the options will not have EMI tax status, but does not of itself take away the optionholder's right to acquire shares under their option agreement.

It is possible, however, for a company to claim a "reasonable excuse" for late filing. If this is accepted by HM Revenue and Customs, EMI status will be permitted.

During the life of an EMI option scheme (that is, until all options have either been exercised or have lapsed or expired), the company must also file an annual return online. This must be done by 6 July following the end of each tax year. A return (a *nil return*) must be filed even if nothing has happened within the scheme during that tax year (e.g. no options have lapsed or been exercised).

### (b) CSOP, SAYE options, and SIP

A company which has established a CSOP, SAYE or SIP scheme must notify HM Revenue and Customs online by 6 July following the end of the tax year in which the scheme was implemented (in other words, when the first option grant or award of shares was made).

As with EMI registrations, this can be done by any group company which has a PAYE reference, and only the company itself can do the registration.

Failure to complete registration on time means that the scheme will not benefit from the intended tax advantages. As with EMI, late registration is permitted where the company can show it has a reasonable excuse.

The company must then file an annual return online in respect of each subsequent tax year. The rules on timing and nil returns for EMI options apply in the same way, and when the scheme has ended it should be closed.

### (c) Other forms of employee share scheme

Any non-tax advantaged (that is, not under EMI, CSOP, SAYE or SIP) award of shares or options to employees or directors must also be notified to HM Revenue and Customs.

This applies to a wide range of arrangements, including (but not limited to):
- *grants of non-approved options*
- *purchases of shares (however they are to be paid for)*

- *awards of free shares*
- *awards of interests in shares.*

This includes shares acquired, or options granted, independently (for example, an employee or director acquiring shares or options from another shareholder).

Registration is only required once there has been a *reportable event*, for example a grant of options or a purchase of shares. A company which establishes a non-approved option scheme but does not immediately grant any options will therefore not yet have anything to notify. Notification must be completed by 6 July following the tax year in which the reportable event occurs and must be completed by the company itself.

Following registration, an annual return must then be filed online annually. The same timings apply as for tax-advantaged schemes and nil returns must still be filed where no reportable events have taken place in the previous tax year. A scheme which has come to an end should be closed; this must be done by the company itself.

### (d) Exercise of options and issues of shares

Whenever a company issues new shares, it must notify the Registrar of Companies. This will be the case both where a company agrees to issue shares directly to any person and where it must do so to satisfy the exercise of an option.

This is done by filing a Form SH01. If the company is registered for online filing with the Registrar of Companies, a paper form is not needed, but otherwise one will be required.

## 20.3 Public information about persons controlling a company: persons with significant control (PSCs) and relevant legal entities (RLE)

Every private company is required to maintain a register of persons with significant control: a *PSC Register*.

This part considers the application of this requirement to a company which is majority owned by an employee trust (whether an employee benefit trust or an employee ownership trust).

To understand how the law in this area works, it is first necessary to understand the meaning of two key terms:

A person with significant control, or *PSC*, is an individual who:
- *holds more than 25% of a company's shares (directly or indirectly) or*
- *holds more than 25% of the voting rights (directly or indirectly) or*
- *holds the right to appoint or remove a majority of the directors (directly or indirectly) or*
- *has the right to exercise, or does actually exercise, significant influence or control over the company or*
- *has the right to exercise, or does actually exercise, significant influence or control of a trust or firm, the trustees or members of which meet any of the above four conditions (or would do if they were individuals).*

Only one of these conditions needs to be satisfied for an individual to be a PSC.

A *relevant legal entity (RLE)* is a legal person (so this can a company, partnership or LLP) that meets both these conditions:
- *it would be a PSC if it were an individual; and*
- *(broadly) it is a company or Limited Liability Partnership.*

### (a) PSC or RLE in relation to the company?
To determine whether the company needs to register a PSC or RLE, it is necessary to consider whether the trust holding shares in it has individual trustees or a single corporate trustee.

Where there are individual trustees, they should not need to register as PSCs as long as none of the five PSC tests above apply to them. However, they will each need to do so if any of them exercise significant influence or control over the trust.

Where there is a corporate trustee, it will need to register as an RLE. Also, if any individual holds a majority of shares in that corporate trustee, they will be regarded as indirectly holding 25% or more of the shares in the company, so will need to register as a PSC.

### (b) PSC or RLE in relation to a corporate trustee?
Where an employee trust has a corporate trustee, it will also be necessary to determine whether it has shareholders or members (if

it is a company limited by guarantee) which need to be registered as a PSC or RLE.

Where, as is commonly the case, its sole shareholder or member is the company, it is arguable that it has no RLE. To identify the company as an RLE would create a circular ownership. If it had individual members or shareholders, any of whom held 25% or more of shares or voting rights, it is likely that they would each be treated as PSCs.

Further, it is considered that directors of a corporate trustee will be considered as PSCs, since they will each be exercising significant influence or control over it.

### (c) A trust with individual trustees
The rules on PSCs and RLEs apply only to companies, so where a trust has only individual trustees, they will not apply.

## 20.4 Accounting

### (a) Employee trusts
How an employee ownership trust is accounted for will be governed by FRS 102 and will depend on the circumstances and structure of the trust.

If an employee trust is considered to be under the control of the employer company in which it holds shares, that company will be required to prepare consolidated financial statements which include the trust. This will generally be the case where an employee trust has been established as a vehicle to provide remuneration to employees, for example by awarding shares to them, and the company de facto is able to decide how those shares should be used. The rationale behind this accounting treatment is that shares held by the trust are to be used to reward employees of the company.

Where an employee trust has a significant long term shareholding in a company and that company does not have power over the trust (for example, it does not have power either to appoint a majority of trustees or to change the trust deed), the generally accepted view is that it is not appropriate to prepare consolidated financial statements including the trust. This would reflect the reality that the trust controls the company and not vice versa. Under this approach, capital contributions by the company to an employee trust would be accounted for in the same way as dividends (although they are not dividends).

## (b) Employee share schemes

Most companies which make a *share-based payment* must record the expense of this in their profit and loss account, also under FRS 102.

A share-based payment includes an award of shares, grant of share options and cash payment where the amount is determined by reference to share value. It includes awards made under both tax-advantaged share schemes and non-tax advantaged share schemes alike.

There are relaxations to this requirement for *small companies* (under the Companies Act 2006) and *micro-entities* (under the Small Companies (Micro-Entities' Accounts) Regulations 2013. See further below.

A company subject to the requirement must determine the fair value of the option or award at the time it is granted or made, and then treat that as an expense in its profit and loss account for the financial period in which the grant or award takes place.

For an award of shares, it will first be necessary to determine the market value of those shares at the time of the award, and then to consider whether any other factors should be taken into account, for example the possibility of those shares being forfeited, before the value of the award itself is identified.

For a share option, its value at the date of grant will generally be a fraction of the market value of the underlying shares, taking various factors into account including:

- *vesting (how long is it until the option can be exercised)*
- *the likelihood of the option lapsing*
- *any performance conditions which must be met as a condition of option exercise, and*

- *volatility: the scope for those shares' value to go up or down for reasons other than company performance (in a private company, this factor may be of limited relevance).*

A small company may choose to prepare accounts under section 1A of FRS 102. This will mean it is only required to comply with the FRS 102 disclosure requirements if they are material, but it will still have to comply with the recognition and measurement requirements (in other words its financial statements will still need to account for the cost but this will not need to be made public).

A micro-entity may choose instead to prepare its accounts under FRS 105. If it does so, it will not be required to account for share-based payments until any shares are actually issued.

**To recap:**
- New offshore trusts must be notified to HMRC.
- It may also be necessary to register a new trust with HMRC under anti-money laundering regulations.
- Employee trusts are subject to certain record keeping requirements.
- Generally, a new employee trust should be notified to HMRC as they may initially wish it to complete a tax return.
- HMRC notification requirements apply to all forms of employee share scheme, and annual returns must also be filed. This is all done online.
- Companies House must be notified of any change in persons with significant control of a company (likely to apply where an employee trust acquires control of a company or at least 25%).
- Consider the accounting treatment of an employee trust. This is likely to depend on whether the trust (i) holds shares intended for employee reward and the company has a strong influence on how those shares are used, or (as is more likely to be the case with employee ownership (ii) the trust holds a majority or significant holding and it is not intended that its shares will be transferred to employees.
- Accounting rules require that the value of share-based payments be shown in a company's accounts.

# Glossary

| Term | Its meaning |
|---|---|
| **Articles of Association** | The core constitutional document of every company. It is a public document as it must be filed at Companies House. Sometimes accompanied by a *shareholder agreement* |
| **Beneficiary** | An individual who can potentially receive benefit from a trust |
| **Company Share Option Plan** | See CSOP options |
| **Corporate trustee** | A company that operates as the single trustee of a trust (instead of the trust having individual trustees) |
| **CSOP options** | Tax- advantaged *share options* (options gains are subject to CGT rather than income tax) |
| **Directors** | The persons responsible for managing a company on a day to day basis |
| **Disguised remuneration legislation** | Anti-avoidance tax legislation targeted at certain financial benefits provided to one or more employees by trusts and other third parties |
| **Disqualifying event** | These can apply to *EMI options,* a *SIP* or to an *employee ownership trust.* They have different triggers but in each case the impact is loss of tax reliefs |
| **EMI options** | Tax- advantaged *share options* (options gains are subject to CGT rather than income tax) |
| **Employee Council** | Often created in an employee-owned company to be the eyes and ears of the trustees, gather and articulate employee ideas, concerns and questions and help feed back to employees from trustees and directors |
| **Employee trust** | Any form of trust which holds shares or other assets for the benefit of employees |
| **Employee benefit trust** | A general form of employee trust under which trustees have wide discretion |

EMPLOYEE OWNERSHIP

| | |
|---|---|
| | how to confer benefit on beneficiaries. Contrast with an *employee ownership trust* |
| **Employee ownership** | Ownership of a company or business (or a substantial part of it) on behalf of all its employees |
| **Employee ownership trust** | A particular form of employee trust under which benefit must be conferred on all employees on the same terms |
| **Employee share scheme** | An arrangement under which one or more employees may personally acquire shares in their company or have shares held on their behalf. Differs from employee ownership which involves ownership of a substantial stake by or on behalf of all employees |
| **Enterprise Management Incentive options** | See *EMI options* |
| **Exercise an option** | See *Option exercise* |
| **Free Shares** | Shares awarded free to employees under a SIP, with no income tax on their value. Can also more generically mean any shares given to an employee |
| **Growth shares** | Shares of a separate class from standard ordinary shares whose value is linked to any growth in value of the company above a pre-set threshold |
| **Hybrid employee ownership** | Employee ownership which combines ownership of shares by both an employee trust and individual employees |
| **Matching Shares** | Free shares awarded to an employee under a SIP which match their agreement to purchase *Partnership Shares* |
| **Nil-paid shares** | Shares which are issued on terms that the purchase price is to be paid later in time. |
| **Non-approved share options** | Share options which do not benefit from tax advantages (so any option gains are subject to income tax on *option exercise* |

| | |
|---|---|
| Option exercise | The exercise by an optionholder of their share option i.e. taking up the right to acquire shares |
| Partnership Shares | Shares purchased by an employee under a SIP, with relief against income tax |
| Perpetuity period | The maximum period under which a trust can exist (unless it is a charitable trust). Currently 125 years. |
| Person with significant control | A person who is able to exercise significant control over a company |
| Phantom shares | A long term cash reward plan which imitates share ownership |
| PSC | See *Person with significant control* |
| Quorum | The number of individuals that must be present at a meeting of directors of trustees in order for the meeting to be validly held |
| Partly-paid shares | Similar to *nil-paid shares*, the difference being that part of the purchase price is paid initially |
| Restricted securities | (Normally) shares which are subject to restrictions e.g. on how they may be transferred |
| Save As You Earn options | See *SAYE options* |
| SAYE options | Tax- advantaged *share options* (options gains are subject to CGT rather than income tax). If granted, they must be offered to all employees on similar terms |
| Shareholder agreement | A contract between a company's shareholders setting out how certain aspects of their relationship will be covered. Many companies do not have one but where they want to agree certain things confidentially they may have a shareholder agreement rather than put these matters in the *articles of association*. |
| Share Incentive Plan | See *SIP* |
| Share options | An option given to an employee (or director or consultant) to acquire shares |

| | in their company |
|---|---|
| **SIP** | A tax-advantaged arrangement under which employees may acquire shares free or purchase them, in each case with relief against income tax. Shares must be offered to all employees on similar terms |
| **Trust** | A legal arrangement under which property is held by a group of persons (*trustees*) for the benefit of others (*beneficiaries*) |
| **Trust deed** | A legal document that creates a trust |
| **Trustees** | The persons holding property under a trust |
| **Unapproved share options** | See *Non-approved share options* |
| **Vesting** | A process under which a person becomes entitled to the full ownership of shares or to exercise options, either over a period of time or on satisfaction of pre-set conditions. |

# Statutory references

# Index

# About the authors

**Robert Postlethwaite** is the founder and managing director of Postlethwaite, a solicitors practice which helps companies throughout the UK and overseas that wish to grow, improve and widen participation in their success through employee ownership and employee share schemes. Robert and his team will design an employee ownership structure or share scheme that matches a company's needs and circumstances, then cover all aspects of its legal implementation.

**Jeremy Gadd** is qualified Coach, Trustee Director and Founder of J Gadd Associates; a business built on the firm belief in the value of working together. He enjoys building powerful relationships with other founders and owners and supporting their business's transition to become employee owned. Here they share the benefits available through building effective engagement, understanding ownership and taking personal responsibility for their success.